THE WAND IN THE WORD

Conversations with Writers of Fantasy

COMPILED AND EDITED BY

Leonard S. Marcus

CANDLEWICK PRESS

Text copyright © 2006 by Leonard S. Marcus
Photography credits appear on page 200.

A Note about the Text:
All bracketed text has been inserted by the editor. Author reading lists are selective, not exhaustive, and reference first U.S. editions only.

First paperback edition 2009

The Library of Congress has cataloged the hardcover edition as follows:

The wand in the word : conversations with writers of fantasy / compiled and edited
    by Leonard S. Marcus. — 1st ed.
    p.   cm.
    ISBN 978-0-7636-2625-9 (hardcover)
    1. Fantasy fiction, American—History and criticism—Theory, etc. 2. Children's
stories, American—History and criticism—Theory, etc. 3. Children's stories,
English—History and criticism—Theory, etc. 4. Fantasy fiction, English—History
and criticism—Theory, etc. 5. Authors, American—20th century—Interviews.
6. Authors, English—20th century—Interviews. 7. Children's stories—Authorship.
8. Fantasy fiction—Authorship.   I. Marcus, Leonard S., date.
PS374.F27W36 2006
813.009'9282—dc22   2005046913

    ISBN 978-0-7636-4556-4 (paperback)

10 9 8 7 6 5 4 3 2 1

Printed in the United States of America

Book design by Lisa Diercks
This book was typeset in Manticore and Gotham.

Candlewick Press
99 Dover Street
Somerville, Massachusetts 02144

visit us at www.candlewick.com

In memory of my mother
L. S. M.

CONTENTS

INTRODUCTION

THIS MIGHT SURPRISE you: until quite recently, fantasy writers were an outcast bunch whose work was rarely prized or rewarded. More often than not, fantasy writers of the past had to defend themselves before a doubting world, to explain why it could possibly make sense for grown persons to spend years creating stories about impossible wizards, witches, dragons, and trolls.

In the course of mounting one such defense, J. R. R. Tolkien singled out for praise fantasy's "quality of strangeness and wonder." Here is our world, a fantasy proclaims, and here is this *other* world, or our own world suddenly seen and experienced from a totally unexpected angle. Fantasy is storytelling with the beguiling power to transform the impossible into the imaginable, and to reveal our own "real" world in a fresh and truth-bearing light. It has the surprising power to make everything it touches upon seem new, unpredictable, and—in Tolkien's fine phrase—"arrestingly strange."

But "many people dislike being 'arrested,'" as the author of *The Lord of the Rings* went on, rather slyly, to observe. While Tolkien immersed himself in writing *The Hobbit* (1937) and *The Lord of the Rings* (1954–55), most members of his generation continued to place their hopes for the future in modern science and technology. Tales of elves, dwarves, and tree people? Ha! Critics wondered why an educated person would waste his time on outmoded make-believe. It was not until late in life that Tolkien had his achievement recognized.

When that finally happened, during the 1960s and early 1970s, things became a bit easier for other fantasy writers as well, although not all at once. Several of the thirteen authors you are about to hear from were early, avid Tolkien fans. Three—Susan Cooper, Diana Wynne Jones, and Philip Pullman—actually crossed paths with the author of the *Rings* trilogy, and tell about it. Several began writing when fantasy was still not just unpopular but widely frowned upon as frivolous or even—terrible term!—"childish." Nobody likes to be called names, but these writers kept on writing anyway. You have to admire their courage.

Tolkien's triumph had a lot to do with the new, more receptive attitude to fantasy that cleared the way for, among other things, the forest-rattling success of Harry Potter. As I recorded these interviews, I began to wonder whether the experience of World War II had not also played a major part in the change. So many of the writers I interviewed had intense, life-altering memories of that war. Several, it seemed, had turned to fantasy both as readers and writers, not to "escape" reality, but as the truest way of coming to terms with wartime terrors that for them lay almost beyond words.

I tape-recorded all but two of the conversations in this collection, some in person and others by telephone. The remaining two interviews were done by e-mail. I asked some questions of all thirteen authors and let other questions be suggested by their individual works and lives. A good interview, like any good conversation, is exploratory in nature, with much of the fun and satisfaction stemming from *not* knowing just where the talk will take you.

While writers don't rely on magical formulas, all experienced word people do have certain habits or rituals or tricks of the trade that work for them, at least part of the time. The authors I interviewed each speak about theirs. If you enjoy writing, you may very well find something of value here to help you on your way. All thirteen are passionate, dedicated professionals who know what they're about. All have funny, serious, and surprising stories to tell.

Let's listen together.

LLOYD ALEXANDER

Born 1924, Philadelphia, Pennsylvania

Died 2007, Drexel Hill, Pennsylvania

LLOYD ALEXANDER is a thoughtful, disarmingly modest man who is quick to see the humor—or folly—in any situation, especially one in which he himself happens to figure. Heroes-in-the-making who think a little too much of themselves, like young Taran at the outset of the Prydain Chronicles, find themselves swiftly—albeit gently—taken down a peg. That *gently* matters: a concern for the way people act and treat one another lies at the core of the drama—whether epic or more humbly scaled—in each of Alexander's stories.

"We can push a button," Alexander once observed, "and light a dozen cities. We can also push a button and make a dozen cities vanish. There is, unfortunately, no button we can push to relieve us of moral choices or give us the wisdom to understand the morality as well as the choices."

Although he considers himself lazy, Alexander has in fact worked exceedingly hard all his adult life. For many years he held down a day job while also writing book after book, starting with three realistic novels and a memoir for adults. Although he is not entirely sure why, starting with *Time Cat,* he turned to writing fantasy, Alexander does know why it was a good choice.

"Hope is an essential thread in the fabric of all fantasies, an Ariadne's thread to guide us out of the labyrinth. . . . Human beings have always needed hope, and surely now more than ever."

Leonard S. Marcus: What kind of child were you?

Lloyd Alexander: I read a lot and I was sick a lot, but I was not the stereotypical bookworm. I also was a good-natured, eager kid. I liked to have fun and to be out exploring. *The Gawgon and the Boy* is absolutely true. The Boy is me at age eleven.

Q: What are some of your first memories of books and reading?

A: All my relatives, with the exception of my dearly beloved aunt Annie, were devout nonreaders. I never saw one of them open a book—ever.

Annie is the Gawgon in *The Gawgon and the Boy.* That's the rest of my family in that book, too, exactly as they were. Annie, who was quite old and frail when I knew her, had been a teacher and was widely read. She introduced me to reading, to poetry, to every good thing like that. And she encouraged me to do what I wanted to do in life—whatever that was.

Although my parents were nonreaders, I did get books from them as presents, as well as from my aunt Annie and on occasion from others. I received books of mythology, *Robin Hood*, and the King Arthur tales, all of which I dearly loved. Chivalry, knightly valor, heroism: I loved it all.

Q: Did you enjoy school?

A: No, unfortunately. I'm very sorry to have to say that. I cannot for the life of me remember any teacher who really encouraged me to do anything. It would be nice to say, "Oh yes, my old high-school English teacher was sure that I would have a glorious career." It didn't happen. I began to write on my own and kept at it out of sheer stubbornness.

Q: Did you go to the public library as a child?

A: There was a library a couple of miles down the road from where we lived. But, no, I never went there. From my parents, I learned early on to distrust all institutions. Stay away from police stations. Stay away from banks. Stay away from public buildings of any kind. They are always sources of trouble. Go to the library? Oh heavens, no. Don't do that!

Q: When did you decide you wanted to be a writer?

A: When I was twelve or thirteen, I wanted to be a poet. I also wanted to be a musician, and at one point I wanted to be an artist. I dearly loved history, and for a while I wanted to be an archeologist, too.

Q: Tell me about your army experiences during World War II.

A: I enlisted because, as a devout antifascist, I felt, This is something I've got to do. I also thought that joining the army would solve all my personal problems. I was at loose ends. I had tried to send myself to college, and I hadn't liked it and quit. I was writing with an enormous

Lloyd Alexander
in uniform
during World
War II

lack of success. So I thought, the army. This answers everything! I
suppose there was the illusion of heroic adventure. I had seen too
many war movies. I imagined there would be a great feeling of com-
radeship and brotherhood. Forget it! It was horrible. For the first time
in my life, I had come up against real power. Our officers literally

could shoot us, no questions asked. I wanted to get out about two minutes after I took the oath. I didn't like the army for some while.

At first they put me in the field artillery, and when I didn't do well, they put me in the band. I played the piano, and because there are no pianos in a marching band, they gave me my choice of bass drum or cymbals. Not being a total fool, I looked at the bass drum and thought, that's *big*. That's heavy. I'll take the cymbals. So I became a cymbal player. But the cymbals were kind of heavy too, and I didn't much like it.

Fortunately, they decided to send me to specialized training in college. It saved my life. We had expert teachers in linguistics, geography, and European history. A few months later, I was transferred to a secret military training center that was one of the most amazing places anyone could have imagined. That's when I finally made some of the best friends I've ever had. We were a fine bunch. We were being trained in five-man teams to parachute into France. We went on maneuvers. We were even shown a staged reenactment of a Nazi rally. As we sat in the audience, "storm troopers" came marching down the aisles carrying banners. Somebody imitated Hitler giving a speech. "Dissenters" were planted in the audience—and were hauled out by the storm troopers. What they were trying to do was show us the psychological climate in which this kind of mob behavior could flourish. It was a powerful experience. Fortunately, our drop was cancelled. Me jumping out of an airplane? I don't think so.

From this training center, we were sent to England and Wales. It was the first time I had ever been that far from home, and here I was in Wales—King Arthur country! I loved the sound of the beautiful

Welsh accent. And I saw castles—things I had only read about—and realized for the first time that, hey, this stuff is real. The impact on me was enormous.

Finally, we were sent to Alsace-Lorraine, in France—and into the real war. From there we went to Germany, in the late spring of 1945, and then, miraculously, I got orders to report to Paris, which was far from the fighting. I had been in combat for just four months, but it felt like a lifetime.

Q: Have your wartime experiences found their way into your books?

A: In many ways. At the beginning of the Chronicles of Prydain, Taran has a naïve idea about what it means to be a warrior—just as I did at first. In *The High King* there is a winter campaign that comes directly from my memories of the bitter cold of the Vosges Mountains of France. In the Westmark trilogy I consciously drew on my memories of the war. The sight of bombed-out towns, of dead animals everywhere—the backwash of the battlefield. The sight of displaced persons pushing handcarts with everything they had in the world. *The Kestrel* is the strongest antiwar book that I've been able to write. It's a brutal book, as it had to be.

Q: You often write about cats too — not just as pets but as friends and even teachers.

A: When I was growing up, we had always had dogs. But my wife insisted on cats, and I was instantly converted. What can I say? I've never seen a cat do a stupid thing—and I can't say the same about human beings. So sometimes I write about the cat as a symbol of reason and common sense. But I'm careful not to overdo this because I dearly love cats for what they are.

Q: Writing the Prydain books must have been an amazing experience.

A: For six years, it occupied almost my every waking thought. I should add that I had a day job at the same time. I worked for a printer, then as a layout artist and advertising copywriter, and finally as an associate editor of an industrial magazine. So I wrote early in the morning and on weekends. Sometimes I would even sneak in a little writing when I had nothing to do at the office.

Q: Your heroes often demonstrate the value of a job well done — even if the job is a lowly one like assistant pig-keeper.

A: I've come to feel that there is no such thing as a lowly job. It's only lowly if a person makes it lowly.

Q: It must have been hard to decide what to write next.

A: I was in tears as I wrote the last couple of pages of *The High King*. I was glad that I had come to the end of six hard years, but a part of my life had also come to an end, and it tore me apart. I had no idea what to do next.

I have always made it a matter of principle not to do the same thing twice. I certainly was not going to try another heroic romance. As I thought about what was most important to me, I thought: I love the music of Mozart. I could hear it playing in my mind, and I decided that I wanted to try to write something "Mozartian," a story set in Mozart's eighteenth-century world. It was a hard thing to do. I completely rewrote *The Marvelous Misadventures of Sebastian* twice.

Q: The magic of Sebastian's violin isn't all good, is it?

A: That's right. The violin is a gift, but an accursed gift. It plays marvelous music, but it will also drain your life. And so the question for him—as it is for anybody who wants to be a musician or artist or writer — is, Is it worth it? Of course, my own answer to that question is *yes*.

Q: Tell me more about the magic in your books.

A: There is usually just one magical element. My principle is the fewer the better. The more magical elements you have, the more likely they are to interfere with each other. If I have a magic mirror, why can't it show me the guy creeping up on me with his magic sword?

Once you have a magical object, the magic has to be limited. If it isn't, you will end up having logical problems. For instance, if you have an invincible weapon, a sword that is completely unbeatable, the story is over. Whoever has it, wins! In the Prydain books, the magic sword cannot be drawn by just anybody but only by someone, as it turns out, who is worthy to be the High King. Otherwise, it's a magic free-for-all.

Q: Do you do research for your books?

A: I have read a great deal about the history of mythology and comparative mythology, and some of my ideas come from the things I've read and learned.

In *The Black Cauldron,* for instance, I took the image of the cauldron capable of magically bringing people back to life from Welsh legend. But then I added the idea that once brought back to life, the warriors would have no memories of themselves as human beings. No remembrance of happiness, kindness, loved ones. That to me is one of the cruelest things I can imagine.

Q: Why do you write for young readers?

A: I have never written with a real child in mind, the way Lewis Carroll did, for example. My daughter was grown up and married by the time I started. I saw the so-called child's book as an art form, and I wanted to try it. I had already tried several other forms—biography and fiction for adults, for instance—and this was another form to try, a form in which I felt there might be hidden possibilities.

Q: Why do you write fantasy?

A: Because, paradoxically, fantasy is a good way to show the world as it is. Fantasy can show us the truth about human relationships and moral dilemmas because it works on our emotions on a deeper, symbolic level than realistic fiction. It has the same emotional power as a dream.

Think of the terrible decision that Taran has to make in *The Black Cauldron,* when the enchantresses say they will trade him the cauldron for the brooch that was given to him by his dear friend Adaon and that allows Taran to have dreams in which the future is revealed. That brooch was a thing of great value. To give that up would be hard, but he did it anyway—for an old cauldron that was going to get destroyed. He was going to turn out the loser no matter what happened. I find the feeling tone of that decision very anguishing, and I would bet that every one of us will go through those same emotions—whatever the specifics of the situation might be—more than once in our lifetime. So I think fantasy does show us the truth of our own lives.

Q: When you start a book, do you know how the story will end?

A: Before I begin writing, I plot my story out in a series of notes. Writing the notes can take months. It's the only way that I have any sense of security. My synopsis is like a blueprint. If I don't have one, the garage is going to end up bigger than the house.

But then what happens—and it always does—is that I will come to a place in the story where I will suddenly realize, This isn't going to work. It's like an explosion. *Bam!* I hate when that happens, and I never get used to it. But I now know why it happens. It's because by the time I reach that point in the story, I am no longer the same person that I was when I began. I have been living my life, having experiences. The experience of writing my notes is in itself an experience! And because I'm not the same person, I see things a little differently—things I hadn't realized earlier.

Q: As you wrote *The Book of Three,* did you know there would be more Prydain books?

A: I thought possibly there would be one more book. At most, two more. But as I continued writing, I saw that I had set things in motion that I had not even realized. At one point I was convinced there would only be four books. I had finished *The Castle of Llyr* and written a first draft of *The High King,* and told my editor that I was done. She said, "Well, that's fine. I have only one suggestion: You have got to write another book!" She saw a gap in the story. At first, I said, "No. I can't do that!" But then I realized she was right, that I needed to give an account of Taran's growing up. And so I wrote *Taran Wanderer.*

That is the book in which Taran, who had hoped he would be a great hero, learns that he is only a human being. When he looks into that pool of water, all he sees looking back is himself: That's what I am—no more, no less. Coming to that realization helps to make him worthy of being the High King. Without that, he wouldn't have been suited for the job. So *Taran Wanderer* was a crucial book.

Q: Do you revise your work much?

A: I rewrite enormously. I've rewritten single pages a dozen times.

Majesty   *later*

"When you left Sundari," Darshan/said to Tamar, "I laid your

sandals on your throne, ~~as I promised, to us,~~ to betoken that you

are still our king. They ~~are still~~ there, *wait* ~~waiting~~ for you! Come   *Ah, enough, enough*

home, lad. You see where this dream of yours has led you." ~~Give you~~

Death, bloodshed, your own life could have been lost

~~up then you can come for it!!!!~~

They had gone to the rooftop terrace ~~of the palace.~~ Beyond

heights of

Ranapura\$ rose the ~~white peaks of~~ the Snow Mountains; ~~and against the~~

leaned on

~~horizon, peaks of Mount Sumeru and Mount Kumeru.~~ Tamar ~~\$\$\$\$\$\$\$\$\$\$~~

the parapet   *fixed*

~~\$\$\$\$\$\$\$\$~~ and ~~turned~~ his eyes to the ~~distant horizon and~~ the   *on*

white peaks of ~~Mount~~ Sumeru and ~~Mount~~ Kumeru. Darshan was watching

of pain   ed   warriors

him; a ~~pleading~~ look\$ shadowing the ~~old soldier's weatherbeaten~~

face.

"Give it up," Darshan urged. *only ill*   *this*

~~Sooner slower in have happily~~ "No ~~good~~ can come of ~~it.~~"

"Once, I would have done so," Tamar said, "and ~~would have~~

done it happily. I even tried to throw away my ring." He shook his

couldn't We'll go into mountains tomorrow.

head. "I can't. ~~I'll never be at peace unless I know for certain~~

~~the other. Mirri made me understand that.~~

"~~What~~, for the sake of a promise you made? Or didn't make?"

is more than honor demands."

Darshan burst out. "This ~~goes beyond honor. It's foolishness!~~

I've seen noble

"Honor?" Tamar said. "I've seen honor lost, dharma ~~broken~~ --

I'm not sure I have even a shred of honor left. Forgotten

my own, as well as others'. No, this is for my own sake. (Mirri

stood

~~made me~~ under~~stand~~ that) A dream? I'll never be at peace until

I know one way or the other. Go back to Sundari, old friend.

This is my last command to you."

I've rewritten chapters two or three times. My first draft is usually a mess. My second draft is a little cleaner.

Q: How do you know when a book is done?

A: I just know. All you *can* know is that this is the best you can do *as of now.*

Q: What is a typical workday like for you?

A: Because I had a day job, I had to train myself to keep to a regular schedule. I still get up at three in the morning, seven days a week, go to my work room, and work three or four hours. Then I stop and see what's going on around the house. I'll go back and look at what I'm doing throughout the day. It's always sort of constantly on my mind.

Q: Has the attitude toward fantasy changed since you've been writing?

A: Oh yes. When I started in the 1960s it seemed that nobody wanted fantasy. People wanted literature to be "relevant," but in a very narrow sense. Now, fantasy is a thriving concern.

Tolkien probably had a lot to do with this. *The Lord of the Rings* was the elephant in the living room. It was so unmistakably a major work that it simply could not be overlooked. People had to say, "Hey, this is great." It may well have opened it up for other fantasy writers.

Q: What do you tell children who want to write?

A: I don't kid them. I tell them that I myself have found it the hardest work that I know. Unless you are willing to make an awful lot of sacrifices for the sake of the work, you may not do as well as you'd like to. It took me seven years before I was published.

Q: What do you like to do for fun?

A: I take my revenge on the world by playing the fiddle. I'm a bad violinist—terrible, despicable. I don't care! And I like to draw cartoons—musical subjects and silly pictures.

Q: What do you like best about being a writer?

A: When I have finished the book and don't have to write it anymore!

A LLOYD ALEXANDER READER

The Chronicles of Prydain:

The Book of Three (Holt, 1964)

The Black Cauldron (Holt, 1965)

The Castle of Llyr (Holt, 1966)

Taran Wanderer (Holt, 1967)

The High King (Holt, 1968)

The Gawgon and the Boy (Dutton, 2001)

The Iron Ring (Dutton, 1997)

The Marvelous Misadventures of Sebastian (Dutton, 1970)

The Rope Trick (Dutton, 2002)

Time Cat: The Remarkable Journeys of Jason and Gareth (Holt, 1963)

The Westmark trilogy:

Westmark (Dutton, 1981)

The Kestrel (Dutton, 1982)

The Beggar Queen (Dutton, 1984)

FRANNY BILLINGSLEY

Born 1954, Chicago, Illinois

WRITING, FOR Franny Billingsley, is slow, laborious, inward-reaching, mysterious work. It entails careful listening to the sounds and rhythms of words and a great deal of puzzling over characters and their choices. It is something like singing, which Billingsley has enjoyed doing since childhood. It is much better than practicing law, which she did for a number of years, at a large Chicago firm, before realizing that writing contracts was not the kind of writing she cared about. Even so, in *Well Wished,* her first book, she was able to call upon her old legal training to craft just the right verbal device for canceling a magic spell gone seriously haywire: "I wish," kindly Mr. Winter intones, "that Catty's body would now be what it would have been if she hadn't made her wish last year."

Determined not to settle for an unfulfilling life, Billingsley also considered becoming a teacher. The same impulse has carried over, in a way, into the work she finally chose. More than anything, writing for her is an experiment in self-teaching and self-discovery. As *The Folk Keeper*'s Corinna, who keeps a diary, reminds herself at a particularly dark time in her young life, "Have I not told myself things through my writing I hadn't thought of before? Hadn't I told myself I could find my way through the Caverns without a candle?"

Leonard S. Marcus: What kind of child were you?

Franny Billingsley: I was a shy, fairly solitary kid. I was not very good at anything, except reading and maybe running the 440-yard dash. I don't think I minded. I lived in a fantasy world.

As a kid, I always had an imaginary story that I told myself in installments. I would lie awake in bed at night—and fall asleep in the middle of it. Sometimes I would tell the story to my younger sister, with whom I shared a room. I also loved to put on plays, and as the oldest, I was always the director and got to play the good parts.

Q: Were there storytellers in your family?

A: As a young man, my father, who grew up in South Dakota, became interested in Scottish ballads. He would listen to his recordings of them over and over again, and then he would sing them to us at night. I'm the oldest of five siblings, and he sang two songs to each of us every night. That's a lot of songs! It was a great gift to us, and I think the Scottish ballads influenced me a lot. They're so haunting and melancholy. Their emotional landscape became part of me from the time I was a little kid. We visited Scotland once when I was seven, and I remember that trip very clearly.

Q: Did you spend much time at the local library?

A: Yes, and my school had a great library. I was a regular.

Q: What did you like to read?

A: I read all kinds of fantasy and novels. Folktales and fairy tales. Edward Eager. C. S. Lewis. E. Nesbit. Then later, big, juicy romantic books like *Jane Eyre* and *A Tree Grows in Brooklyn*.

Q: Were you a good student?

A: Actually, I was a terrible student. I didn't do my homework, and I mostly got C's. My parents, who were pretty relaxed in some ways, let me not be a good student. I really appreciated that they didn't bug me about not studying. I find now that as a parent I'm much more of a busybody!

Q: Corinna is very feisty. Were you like that too?

A: I think she is the girl I wanted to be. Besides being shy, I was always cowed by authority. Even now, when I'm driving, if I see a policeman behind me, I get nervous! I never made a disturbance. I followed the rules. Corinna's big thing is that she wants power, and I suspect that as a child I wanted power too, and maybe felt very disempowered. But I didn't have the courage to argue for it.

Q: When did you begin to write?

A: In addition to always being the best reader in the class, I did quite a bit of writing as a child. I wrote haiku, and I wrote lots of limericks—funny poetry. I remember starting to write a novel when I was about twelve. But it never occurred to me that I could make a career and a life out of reading and writing.

Q: Were there teachers who encouraged you?

A: No, there weren't. I went to a fancy private school, but no one there really got who I was. That again was probably in part due to my being such a quiet kid. There was one English teacher, in eleventh grade, who would occasionally look at a journal I kept that year, in which I doodled a lot and wrote poems. He *was* encouraging and would say things like, "You have a real ear for words and a great sense of humor." He was the only one who ever suggested that I might live a life of words.

Then there came a time, just as I was graduating from high school, when things reversed themselves and it became important to me to somehow prove to the world that I was a competent person. I drew away from reading and became pretty obsessed with doing well in school and embracing outward measures of success. And I think that led inexorably to my becoming a lawyer. In doing so, I had left my true interest, which was reading, behind—though of course I would not have phrased it to myself that way then.

Q: What was it like being a lawyer?

A: For me it was so boring. It was stressful, and often the people were not very nice. I hated going to work in the morning.

Q: Then what happened?

A: I was in my fifth year, had begun to look for other jobs, and was feeling pretty desperate, when I visited my sister, who was living in Barcelona. She was teaching English and had almost no money. But she had a lot of time. I was just the opposite: I had lots of money

certain that this was the end of my own true skin, the one I'd
been wearing for seventeen years, which I'd often scorned,
longing to be one of those rosy young ladies, walking down the
streets of Rhysbridge. It now seemed infinitely precious to me.
I could feel the heat from all those bodies, hear the soft
panting, and wondered what they were waiting for, what secret
signal were they waiting for before they leapt upon me.

I looked up at last from those warm, writhing pool, vowing
that if I got out of this alive I'd save my skin and leave
Mirblehaugh Park at once. I would not have thought it would be
possible to be more frightened, but it was. My heart beneath my
folded hands gave an odd lurch when, in the mirror over the
mantle, I met my father's eyes.

He might have been looking at me for some time in the
mirror, as I stood starting down at the dogs. He sat in a wing
chair, its back towards me, facing the hearth. He must have been
staring into the dark, cold fireplace. I could see almost all of
him in the big mirror, as he must, then, be able to see me. Flat
gray skin over knife-sharp cheekbones. Not so much pale, as
simply bleached of all color. I realized I'd expected some fat-
faced gentleman with red veins in his nose. Stained gray hair
that might once have been red, colorless eyes, pale lips, opening
now--

"So this is the Scrap Edward has been telling me about?"
Mainland voice, but which had, after so many years, begun to take
on the lilt of the Northern Isles.

Franny
Billingsley,
age ten, with
a parakeet
on her head

and no time. My sister had time to go on walks, time to talk to her friends! That opened my eyes. I thought, What the heck am I doing? Four months later, I quit my job and moved to Barcelona, taking along with me all my favorite children's books, including *Harriet the Spy* and *A Wrinkle in Time,* as well as some new books that someone had recommended—Robin McKinley's *Beauty* and Lois Lowry's

Anastasia Krupnik. I don't think I knew just why I brought those books. But when I started reading them, I found myself asking myself, How could I have gotten so far from what I really love? I felt that I had come full circle: back to the kid who was always reading. Back to the delicious world of fantasy and emotion—a world I valued. I thought, I'm back home! Once I made that connection, I thought, Maybe I'll try to *write* a children's book. That was in 1983. I stayed in Spain for two and a half years. I wrote a bunch of terrible things. Then in 1988 I started *Well Wished*. It was published in 1997.

Q: That was a long time.

A: By then, I had moved back to Chicago, taken a wonderful course in children's literature, and found a job at a bookstore, which I loved. I also joined a writers' group, which has been fantastic. There are six of us, and we give each other a chance to look at what we've written in a fresh way.

Q: Your stories are mysterious. You make it a little hard, at first, for readers to find their way in. . . .

A: I do love mystery. But I try to make my writing as clear as I can. In fact, I hate puzzles. I hate mazes. I hate playing Scrabble! I know that my stories are complicated, and I hope that as I grow as a writer, I will find ways to make them not less mysterious but more accessible.

Q: What about the game of Description, which Nuria plays in *Well Wished*? Did you play that game as a child?

A: Not, like Nuria, with another person. But I was a very romantic kid. And as I've already said I always wrote poetry. So in a way I did play Description with myself.

Q: Why do you think you write fantasies instead of some other kind of story?

A: Fantasy is romantic in nature. It's filled with silks and satins and daggers—and the possibility of wonderfully challenging transformations. How interesting it is to me to try to describe a person who is being taken over by her seal skin, or who can sense the world around her through her hair. That to me is fascinating.

Also, fantasy allows you to step outside our world and look at it with a little bit of perspective. It can take something in our world, for instance "identity," which has only an abstract reality, and it can make it palpable. Both of my books are attempts to grapple with identity. I have used a literal vehicle—a physical skin—for my characters to explore who they are beneath their skin, what skin they belong in. Corinna thinks she's a Folk Keeper but really she's a seal maiden. Where is her seal skin? What's she going to do with it? Will it fit her emotionally as well as physically? Will it take her into the sea? And if it does, what will she decide to do once she's there? So, there's a connection between the inner story—the story of who she is—and the outer story—which is the story of her physical identity. So that for me is what fantasy can do so well.

Q: Do you have a daily work routine?

A: My best time to write is in the early morning. I try to write four hours a day, starting around 5:30. But because my husband, a professor of English and theater, also finds that the morning is the best time for writing and class preparation, we switch off days. When it's not my turn, I get the kids off to school and do my writing later.

I write in longhand. Later in the day I may transcribe what I've written into the computer.

Q: How do you get started with a book?

A: I start with an idea for what I call the "complication" of a story. Wouldn't it be interesting to have two kids switch bodies? Especially, one kid who's active, energetic, and outdoorsy and another who can't walk. What would that be like? Or—what if there were a girl who was half selkie, half human? At first she doesn't know what her heritage is. Once she does know, what will she decide is the right place for her? At this stage, I have no idea what my character's name is, how old she is, what the setting is going to be.

Q: Do you make an outline?

A: I'm a plunger, not an outliner. So I jump in with both feet and kind of swim around in what at first is a very dark sea. For *Well Wished*, it took me about three years before I came up with the idea of the Well. It took me all that time to find what the magical device would be through which the kids switch bodies. Originally, I had cast the character of Agnes as a witch who casts a spell. But that seemed a little thin and unsatisfactory. Why would she do that? Why wouldn't she cast a spell to switch them back? The idea that Nuria would break a rule and get herself into trouble seemed deeper and more connected to Nuria's character.

Q: Do you do research for your books?

A: Although the Folk are my creation, they're clearly drawn in part from fairy-tale and folktale creatures like goblins and trolls. In order to figure out what the Folk might be all about, and what their powers and limitations were going to be, I used a wonderful book called *An Encyclopedia of Fairies* by Katharine Briggs, which is all about Celtic creatures. I came upon interesting details: that cold iron is a protection against fairies, which is why Corinna wears a necklet of nails. Under *L* in this encyclopedia is an entry for "The Last Word." It states that when a fisherman puts out to sea, he may be accosted by evil sea spirits, which would seek to sink his ship. They would have a kind of duel with rhyming words, and whoever got the last word won. If it was the fisherman, then the ship was safe.

Q: How do you go about naming your characters?

A: Naming characters for me is very difficult. Nuria was going to be Sara at first, I think because I wanted her to be like Sara Crewe in Frances Hodgson Burnett's *A Little Princess*. But then I realized that because I needed this book to have a faraway and long-ago and misty feeling, Sara was too familiar-sounding a name. Then the name Nuria came to me. It's a name from Spain, and it sounded kind of romantic, and it is pronounced the way it's spelled, so it seemed perfect.

At first I called Corinna Fiona. But Fiona is a common Scottish name, and I didn't want people to think of the story as being set in Scotland, or anywhere in particular. I tried Marisa, Rhyanna. Then I went through books of baby names and found the name Corinna, which felt just right. In it is the word *core*, and during the course of the novel, Corinna finds out who she truly is—she finds her core.

Q: Do you revise your work?

A: I think best when my pen is moving across the page in the act of trying to tell my story. So I write volumes and volumes and volumes of pages. After I finish a draft or two, I look at it and say, "Okay. What have we here? What can I use? What do I need to be thinking about? What do I have to jettison?" It's usually a lot! Images come to me in great vats of words, and I have to kind of sand them down until I'm left with a single, shining image and not something that gets in the way of my plot. In *Well Wished,* I came up with the game of Description out of a desire to keep some of the descriptions that I really liked but which didn't otherwise fit into my plot. The game turned out to serve the story well, too.

If, as I'm writing, I have ideas for a later chapter, I write them down on note cards and put them in a box. Then as I come to each new chapter, I'll look at the cards in the box for anything useful. It's a messy process! And it takes me a very long, long time.

Q: Has your experience as a lawyer helped you as a writer?

A: It may have taught me to think clearly and to be willing to heartlessly strip away the stuff that doesn't serve my story.

Q: Do you, like your character Corinna, keep a diary?

A: I did as a child. Sometimes now I'll keep journals of particular experiences I want to remember. I was once in Wyoming, for instance, and on the plane back to Chicago there were lots of people going to a rabbit breeders' convention. Everyone on the plane was talking about rabbits. "How long is the fur of your lop-eared blah, blah, blah." On the runway, as I looked out the window, I could see tons of crates of rabbits being loaded onboard. It was hilarious. I like to write down those moments because who knows if I'll use them in a book or not.

Q: What do you tell children who want to write?

A: Sometimes when I talk to groups of kids, I walk them through the process of writing *The Folk Keeper.* I show them early drafts, for instance, and talk about why they don't work and what it took to make Corinna come alive as a character. I also give workshops in which we develop characters and write beginnings of stories and try to create a believable world. I try to leave them with the idea that writing is mostly about perseverance. It is the people who just don't give up who get published.

Q: What is the best part of being a writer?

A: Writing connects me with myself. This is what I most love about it, although it's sometimes easy to forget because writing is so horribly hard—like digging in a quarry with a butter knife. But I always miss it if I'm away from it for too long. In some ways, it's a little like exercise (my goal is to run four times a week). It's hard to get to the gym—sometimes I even dread it—but I always love having run, and I miss it if I don't. And sometimes, often when I least expect it, some surprising energy overtakes me and I run like the wind (a rather slow wind, but that doesn't make it any less fun!). The same is true of writing. Sometimes—and again, often when I feel most sluggish—words flow out the end of my pen, whole scenes come together, characters begin to crackle and shine. It's the most exciting thing I can think of. And just as running connects me with my physical self, writing connects me with my emotional self; I can think of no better thing than that.

A FRANNY BILLINGSLEY READER

The Folk Keeper (Jean Karl/Atheneum, 1999)

Well Wished (Jean Karl/Atheneum, 1997)

SUSAN COOPER

Born 1935, Burnham, Buckinghamshire, England

S USAN COOPER has always paid close attention to her dreams. In one dream that she has never forgotten, she is alone and reading in a library when one of the library walls suddenly falls away to reveal a crowded theater, its audience gazing in her direction. The image seems a powerful description of a life spent in large part writing books, plays, and television and film scripts that have won for their author—an essentially private person—legions of readers and fans.

Cooper moved to the United States in 1963 to marry an American college professor and has lived in New England more or less continuously ever since. In her fantasy novels, however, she has returned time and again to the landscapes that she affectionately calls her "places"—the sights and settings not only of her own childhood but also of the Arthurian and Celtic myths and legends with which she feels an even more fundamental kind of connection.

Fantasy writers, Cooper once observed, "live in the same world" as everyone else. "But we perceive [it] differently. We see around corners"—sharing a deep curiosity about "myth, legend, folktale; the mystery of dream, and the greater mystery of Time. With all that haunting our minds, it isn't surprising that we write stories about an ordinary world in which extra-ordinary things happen."

Leonard S. Marcus: What kind of child were you?

Susan Cooper: Terribly shy. I did a lot of solo bicycle riding from about the time I was ten. I was a very bookish child, and I began writing very young, too. I was the kind of child who wrote for the school magazine and ended up editing it. Then later I edited the Oxford University newspaper, which was the first time a woman had done it.

Q: Time is a riddle and a mystery in your books. In *Silver on the Tree,* for instance, Merriman tells Will, "All times coexist, and the future can sometimes affect the past." Do you remember learning to tell time?

A: No, but I remember being sent at the age of six to look at the school clock, and coming back to tell the teacher what time it was, and being deeply embarrassed because I had to say, "Well, the big hand is on five and the little hand is on two." So I can remember *not* being able to tell time.

I remember my *sense* of time then. Children are very conservative. I remember thinking that the way things are is the way they should stay and feeling ridiculously angry, for instance, when I was about eight, when somebody tarmacked a road that had been white.

I grew up in Buckinghamshire, surrounded by ancient things. As a child I had a sense of a very layered history. I took for granted the fact that a farmer could be plowing his field and find a Roman pavement; that I could see Windsor Castle, which goes back to Norman times, from my bedroom window; that there was an Iron Age fort on the way to school. It was just a mound; nevertheless, it was an Iron Age fort.

Q: What do you remember about World War II?

A: I was four years old when the war broke out and ten when it ended. We lived very close to the main railway line, and the Germans were always trying to bomb it. So we had an anti-aircraft post at the top of the road. The public air-raid warning was an up-and-down wailing sound, and to this day I jump whenever I hear an ambulance siren. But the guys at the anti-aircraft post had their own signal—a hammer hitting a pipe, a kind of hollow sound, and sure enough, whenever you heard that, you would hear the wailing siren about five minutes later.

It was a childhood of noises and concerned adults. My father worked in an office in London, which was twenty-three miles away, and some nights he wouldn't come home because he was fire-watching on the roof of Paddington Station. The Germans dropped incendiary bombs, which were designed specifically to make things catch fire, and so he and others would be up on the roof dousing the bombs with water before they could burn the place down. Going to school, we had a school bag on one shoulder and a gas mask on the other. We collected shrapnel from bomb craters. It was a status symbol to have a big collection of shrapnel! And everything was rationed: food, fuel, paper. Rationing continued for another six years after the war, into my adolescence.

Q: Was the war terrifying? Or did it seem exciting to you as a child?

A: As children, we didn't know enough to be frightened. For us the war was normal: we'd never known anything different. And yes, it was exciting.

The first time I can remember being afraid was during an air raid. Planes were fighting overhead as we ran from the house to the air-raid shelter, which was under the back lawn. I remember being fascinated, and pausing to look up, and my very gentle father suddenly reaching out and grabbing me down into the shelter. Because he was frightened, I became frightened too.

I think the whole Light and Dark thing in the Dark Is Rising books goes back to my being a child during the war. We thought in terms of "good guys" and "bad guys." We were so soaked in it that we didn't have to be taught to feel that way. It was a kind of prejudice, really, and after the dropping of the atomic bombs by the Americans, I realized that the good guys could do bad things too. And so I think the books try to say that extremism of any sort is bad and that at either end of the spectrum you are in danger of damaging people.

Q: Were there good storytellers in your family?

A: My younger brother and I were always asking our parents to tell

Susan Cooper,
age three

us stories about life before the war. Or we would say, "Tell us about the olden days," by which we meant when they were children. And I had a grandfather who lived two bus rides away, and there would occasionally be a big family party where Grandfather would recite long poems or do monologues—things he'd heard in the old English music halls.

My grandfather was stage-struck. He used to take his children—including my mother when she was young—to the theater to see an actor he very much admired named Henry Lytton. To the children's great embarrassment, Grandfather would jump to his feet and shout "Bravo!" when it was time to applaud, and after the performance he would take them round to the stage door so that he could raise his hat to Henry Lytton.

Years later, Grandfather took me to see a film called *Stairway to Heaven*. It was a fantasy that told two stories at once. The "real" story was set during World War II. The film was really about life and death, and it had such a profound impact on me that I knew it almost by heart, frame by frame.

Q: Did you like to read?

A: Oh yes. Folktales, myth, fairy stories: everything in that pot fed my imagination. Not too many books were being published during the war years, so you had to make do to some extent with the books that happened to be on the shelves at home. I remember picking my way through a twenty-volume set of Dickens by the time I was eight. The readable bits, you know! Radio opened all sorts of imaginative doors too. I remember an hour-long program at five o'clock, called *Children's Hour*, that did dramatizations of books that I hadn't read and wouldn't otherwise have read because I had no way of getting at them, particularly John Masefield's *The Box of Delights* and *The Midnight Folk*. Magic! There was no public library in reach, and I didn't go to a school with a library until I was ten. Once I found that, it was wonderful, a treasure cave!

Q: When did you start to write?

A: I wrote and illustrated my first story when I was about eight. I had put it in a drawer, and my favorite uncle found it and read it, and came to me and said, "This is very good!" I was so appalled that I burst into tears, snatched the book away, and tore it up—because it was supposed to be private.

When I was fourteen, I started to write a memoir called *Fourteen*. I thought that adults had absolutely forgotten what it was like to be fourteen, and I was going to remind them. But I kept not finishing it, and after a while the title had changed to *Sixteen*! And I gave up.

Q: Did anyone besides your uncle offer you encouragement?

A: My mother, who was a teacher, and my father, who worked for the Great Western Railway, both liked to read. They encouraged me and let me know that they expected me to do well.

Q: Were you a good student?

A: Horribly good! History was my best subject, even better than English. That was probably just because I had a very good memory. By the time I went to university, I knew I was going to study English because I couldn't imagine living without it. In high school, for about two weeks, I had considered studying science instead—because I had a crush on the physics teacher! But then I thought, No, no, no. I can't

Bird

Snake

rubbed, polished stone

lonely pilgrimage

GREENWITCH

Chapter One

Only one newspaper carried the story in detail, under the headline TREASURES STOLEN FROM MUSEUM.

"Several Celtic works of art were stolen from the British Museum yesterday, one of them worth more than £15,000. Police say that the theft must have taken place during opening hours, with the help of skeleton keys, since the showcases involved were totally undamaged.

"The missing objects include a gold chalice, three jewelled brooches and a bronze buckle. The chalice, known as the Trefgosick Grail, had been acquired by the Museum only last summer, after its dramatic discovery in a deep cave by three children. It had been valued at £15,000, but a Museum spokesman said last night that its true value was "incalculable."

"He added that the Museum appealed to the

do this! So I switched. After I graduated from Oxford, at the age of twenty-one, I went knocking on doors in London and was eventually taken on as a journalist by the Sunday *Times*.

Q: While at Oxford, did you meet J. R. R. Tolkien?

A: I never met him, but I went to his lectures on Anglo-Saxon literature, along with hundreds of other students. He was a wonderful lecturer. Like C. S. Lewis, whose lectures I also attended, he was a tweedy, pipe-smoking, middle-aged man. We were all waiting for the third volume of *The Lord of the Rings* to come out. The grandeur of the whole concept—the scale of the books—impressed me. Also, Tolkien's strong sense of place. I loved Gollum. And I loved the sense of Frodo as a very small person pitted against this huge might of evil. That certainly must be one of the things behind the patterning of the Dark Is Rising books.

Q: Did you like writing for a newspaper?

A: I had a wonderful time, met all kinds of people, got into all kinds of situations. But I also got frustrated because I wasn't using my imagination. Then at the suggestion of one of the editors, I entered a publisher's competition to write a "family adventure story." I went to work on it, but within two chapters, my book had stopped being an adventure story and become a fantasy, and I'd met Merriman, my Merlin figure. And so I thought, To heck with the prize. I was into the story, which became *Over Sea, Under Stone*. And my imagination said, "Thank you!" because this was what I really wanted to be writing.

Q: Did you know when you wrote *Over Sea, Under Stone* that it was going to be the first book in a series?

A: No. I left *Over Sea, Under Stone* sort of open-ended because I didn't want to leave the people forever, but I had no idea whether I was going to write any more about them. Meanwhile, my life changed totally. I married an American and went to live in America, where I wrote other kinds of books—a biography, a book about America, a memoir.

Then one day while I was out cross-country skiing, I suddenly knew as I was looking at the snow that I was going to write a book about a boy who wakes up on his eleventh birthday and finds he can work magic. And I thought, The setting is going to be English, but the snow is going to be like this. Then I tried to write that book, and it didn't come out well at all. So that went into the back of the head. Then there was this peculiar day in my little study at the top of the house. The children were in school, I suppose. I'd been re-reading *Over Sea, Under Stone,* and I suddenly thought, This is it. This is the beginning, and *that* boy—Will Stanton—who wakes up and goes out into the snow, he's part of that same story. Then it was like having pressed some magic key. I found there would be five books. I wrote down the titles of the next four books, and where they were going to be set and at what times of year, and very, very roughly who was going to be in each of them. And I wrote the last page of the last book and put it away.

Q: And then you wrote the second book, *The Dark Is Rising*?

A: Yes. Eight years had gone by since *Over Sea*. I was extremely home-sick, and the landscapes of the last four books are all my places in England. I would go into them in my head, even though I was actually sitting in Winchester, Massachusetts.

Q: What are some of those places?

A: First, Buckinghamshire, where I grew up and where Will Stanton and his family live. And then mid-Wales, which is where my grand-mother came from and where we would spend holidays. I'm one-quarter Welsh, and I've always been obsessed by the place—by the fact that the earliest people of Britain went west to Wales, driven back by successive waves of invaders from the continent. The Picts, the Celts, the Gaels—they were all driven back by Romans, Angles, Saxons, Vikings, Normans. I think the Welsh part of me is very powerful, and to this day when I go to Wales, I feel I'm going home.

My third place is Cornwall, where we think my father's family came from and where we also spent holidays when I was a kid. The history of Cornwall is more or less the same as that of Wales. The early people got driven into that little peninsula as well. So, there are these blood ties. And if there were such a thing as the Old Magic, these are the places—Wales, Cornwall—where it would be.

For some peculiar reason I've never written a story set in the United States, where I live. The Boggart books are set in Toronto and Scotland, both places I'm fond of, and *Green Boy* is about a Bahamian island I've loved for twenty-five years. *King of Shadows* does start in Massachusetts, but then it zooms off to London. Maybe next time . . .

Q: Do you have a daily work routine?

A: After breakfast, if I'm writing a book, I'll take a pad of paper and a pen, shut myself in the bedroom, turn off the telephone, sit on the floor, and write. There has to be a lot of slightly magical stuff beforehand: I have to read what I wrote the day before; I have to walk about. You are really doing these things in order to put yourself into a kind of trance state. It's partly a way of avoiding getting down to it, but it's also a way of getting yourself out of real life and into the place where the words come from. And so I will sit there with my pad—often it's a hardback notebook—and my pen and write until lunchtime. If it doesn't go well, then I will go out for what I call a "thinking walk." But if it does go well, I come to a point after about three hours when I stop.

A thousand words a day would be a very good day for me. I will be writing on one side of the notebook and talking to myself on the other: making notes and asking myself questions. When I think I'm getting to the end of the morning's work, I will start talking to myself about what comes next so that I'll know where I'm going when I start again. After lunch I'll go to my study with the notebook and put what I've written in longhand into the computer. It changes as I go, and sometimes I find myself going on ahead, which is lovely. Then I print it out so I've got it to read the next morning. And so it grows, very gradually.

Q: Do you know from the start how a book will end?

A: I know the start and I know the end but I know very little about the middle.

Q: Do you do research for your books?

A: A huge amount. I have shelves of books on all sorts of obscure subjects. When I was writing *Over Sea, Under Stone,* for instance, I needed to know about a certain type of rock formation found in Cornwall called a *fogou.* It's a kind of tunnel going down from the surface of the earth. I wanted my kids to be able to reach the beach from a headland, so I got very involved in looking up fogous. *King of Shadows,* a book about a modern boy actor who finds himself in Shakespeare's company in 1599, took a year of reading about Elizabethan England

and two backstage visits to the rebuilt Globe Theatre in London. Detail is important.

In *Silver on the Tree,* there's a moment where Jane is up at sunrise and is out on the dunes and the beach in Aberdyfi, where my parents lived. I thought, I'd better get this right. So the next time I was home in Wales, I got up before sunrise and went out onto the dunes with my little notebook. I could have described the dunes and the beach from memory. But there were some details I couldn't have remembered: the length of shadow, the colors at the moment of sunrise.

Q: Do you revise your work?

A: Not a great deal. Once I have the rough draft, I will go through it very carefully and read it and read it and read it, and talk to myself on paper about what doesn't work and what does. And then I will start again, this time on the computer, and produce what you might call the smooth draft. That tends to be the one that goes to the editor.

I said before that I wrote down the titles of the last four books in the series all at once. Two of the titles later changed, though. *The Dark Is Rising* was going to be called *The Gift of Gramarye*—*gramarye* being an old word for magic—but my editor thought it sounded too much like grammar. *The Grey King* was going to be called *Fire on the Mountain,* but at the last minute we found out that someone had just published a collection of Haitian folktales with that same title.

Q: What do you tell young people who say they want to write?

A: To those up until the age of about fifteen, I say, Read, read, read.

Write if you feel like it. But reading—getting the words and the rhythms inside you—is the most important thing, because you'll never have so much time again.

Q: What do you like best about being a writer?

A: Being able to go into this other place and live there for a while. Writing the kinds of stories I like to read. But mostly it's the sense of discovery, which you don't get every day in real life.

A SUSAN COOPER READER

The Boggart books:

The Boggart (Margaret K. McElderry/Atheneum, 1993)

The Boggart and the Monster (Margaret K. McElderry/ Atheneum, 1997)

The Dark Is Rising sequence:

Over Sea, Under Stone (Margaret K. McElderry/Atheneum, 1965)

The Dark Is Rising (Margaret K. McElderry/Atheneum, 1973)

Greenwitch (Margaret K. McElderry/Atheneum, 1974)

The Grey King (Margaret K. McElderry/Atheneum, 1975)

Silver on the Tree (Margaret K. McElderry/Atheneum, 1977)

Green Boy (Margaret K. McElderry/Atheneum, 2002)

King of Shadows (Margaret K. McElderry/Atheneum, 1999)

The Magician's Boy, illustrated by Serena Riglietti (Margaret K. McElderry/Atheneum, 2005)

NANCY FARMER

Born 1941, Phoenix, Arizona

T HE WORLD," writes Nancy Farmer, "is composed of great sorrow and great joy. It has a grandeur beyond anything I can describe, but this I can say: to know what you are and where you belong is the true meaning of Magic."

Farmer gamely puts these wise words in the mouth of Rodentus, the roguish, well-traveled rat who, in her novel *The Warm Place*, befriends a runaway giraffe anxious to find her way home to Africa from a zoo half a world away. Like the determined heroine of that fantasy, Farmer herself has heeded the rat's advice, venturing far and wide in pursuit of self-knowledge. Born in the American Southwest, she has lived in India, where she served as a Peace Corps volunteer, and in Africa as well as in Oregon and California. She worked as a research scientist for many years before surprising herself one day with the realization that writing fiction was her true vocation.

Farmer's ambitious, quirky, compassionate novels range widely across time, geography, and the world's cultures, mixing elements of mythology, fantasy, fable, science fiction, and realism. A reader might well wonder how it is that someone with this author's scientific training ever came to write stories in which talking animals, surrealistic mutants, medicine men, and the spirits of the dead all figure as characters. Once again, it is Rodentus who knows: "Why the world is steeped in Magic," says the rat. "A seed of it lies at the heart of every living thing."

Leonard S. Marcus: What kind of child were you?

Nancy Farmer: I was a solitary child, in part because my brother and sister were a lot older than I was. When I was young, we had a yard where I mostly played with animals. I had chickens. I put out water so that the desert animals, such as roadrunners, would come in. Once we got a wildcat, but it ate the chickens, so that wasn't so successful. I played a lot with bugs.

My parents were against having dogs or cats, and when they told my brother and me that we could have anything else, my brother went out and got scorpions to raise, and I got black widow spiders! I also had a pet tarantula that escaped in my bedroom. When I couldn't find him, I put pans of water under all the legs of my bed so he wouldn't crawl in with me.

Eventually, my parents did let me have a dog—and that is when I learned to bark. I was very interested in communicating with animals.

There are several kinds of barks—a challenge bark and a call saying, "I'm here. Please answer," and a friendly call. I learned those. And when we moved to the hotel my father managed in Yuma, Arizona, my parents let me "keep" alley cats—I wasn't supposed to have any animals at the hotel—so long as the cats stayed in the alley. At one time, I had eighteen. I named them all after volcanoes, and I used to go out and watch them a lot—their behavior and politics. And I learned how to do several cat calls, how to get cats to come to me.

I've always been interested in animals. In Africa I sat and watched monkeys. If you sit still long enough, they'll come down out of the trees to inspect you. I've had them feel my hair, but I had to be careful about it. An excited monkey can pull your hair out by the roots, even a small one. I put a scene like this in *A Girl Named Disaster*.

Q: Did you like to read?

A: Oh yes, I read all kinds of things. The Oz books of course. Devoured every one of them. I read fairy tales. But I also read comic books like *Captain Marvel* and *Classic Comics* and *Donald Duck*. My parents had a good library and because I was alone so much, I got to reading Maupassant and Victor Hugo at a really early age. Then I got to the age when you want to read about sex and I read a lot of books because I thought there was going to be *something* in them, and which turned out for other reasons to be pretty good—*Canterbury Tales,* for instance. My parents told me I mustn't read that because it had naughty stuff in it. I think they knew all along what they were doing!

Q: Were there storytellers in your family?

A: My grandfather had a newspaper for which he wrote news articles. My father was a very good storyteller but he was afraid of rejection slips, so he never got anything published. Then there was my mother, who wanted to be a writer without actually having done anything. She was basically lazy, though she did write an autobiography of her childhood, which I have. My sister started writing, but she never did it much.

Q: Were you good at school?

A: I failed the first two grades because I was dyslexic and nobody knew what was wrong with me. I couldn't hold a pencil properly. I couldn't tell left from right, so I did mirror writing. I didn't get any good grades until around the end of third grade. After that, I did okay—except that I was so bored in school that I would daydream all the time. Then in seventh grade, I started playing hooky, and after two years of that, I was sent to a church school to try and straighten me out. It didn't work. I was thrown out of that school for instigating a riot in the middle of the night. First we threw the headmistress out in the snow, broke open the Coke machine and drank all the Coke, and rolled toilet paper down the stairs. Then we stood up on the roof, yelled to the boys' dormitory, took off our shirts, waved them in the air, and invited the boys over. After that, I was no longer welcome at that school. I was kind of a wild kid.

But I loved college. At Reed College, I was part of what they called their "eccentric quota"—students they took in because we had some talent but were also so weird that we wouldn't have fit in anywhere else.

Q: When did you first read *The Lord of the Rings*?

A: After returning from the Peace Corps in India, I lived in a hippie commune and one of the men in the house gave me the first book,

Nancy Coe, about age six, with her brother Elmon Lee Coe, mugging for the camera

The Fellowship of the Ring. I read it in one sitting and I just couldn't believe what a great book it was. At the end, Gandalf falls into the mines of Moria, and so at about midnight I went to this guy's room and I banged on his door and said, "What happened to Gandalf?" He opened the door and said, "If I tell you, it will be a cop-out!" and he closed his door and locked it. I was devastated because I really, really had to know—and that was a problem because he didn't have the second book. *Nobody* in the commune had the second book! So I had to wait until after work the next day and run to the bookstore and buy *The Two Towers.*

The Lord of the Rings still seems to me to be one of the most remarkable books I've ever read. I read it again occasionally just to get the feel of the language. *The Sea of Trolls* is based on Norse sagas, and I hope it honors the tradition that Tolkien started.

Q: What kind of scientific work did you do?

A: First I worked for a lab in Berkeley, California, making bubonic plague vaccine. That was a short-term job, and it wasn't very satisfactory because I went to work before dawn and left for the day after dark and there weren't any windows in the lab. I found it very depressing. Then I went to work for the entomology department at the University of California at Berkeley. That was a great job because my task was to control insects that ate traffic islands in

California. I traveled all over the state, worked with road crews, told them the good bugs from the bad bugs, and told them when to spray and when not to spray. My boss at the university used a lot of biological controls so they wouldn't have to use chemicals. That was a very nice job—until I got promoted and had to stay in an office and tell other people to go out and do all the fun stuff. That's when I decided to go to Africa.

After putting together a list of African entomologists, I bought a ticket on a freighter bound for Cape Town, South Africa. My plan was to walk up to the nearest entomologist and ask for work. My first job involved traveling all around South Africa. Then I got my dream job, up in Mozambique, for which I went around Lake Cabora Bassa by boat every two weeks to check the waterweeds and check if the water was safe for people to drink. That was where I got most of my information for *A Girl Named Disaster*. My lab assistant Malisani had a lot of enemies, and he invited witch doctors over to get charms or curses. I learned a lot from Malisani and also from the witch doctors. There were the good witch doctors, the ones who heal people, but there were also a few of the bad kind who could give you poison or rent out a vampire to get your enemies.

Q: When did you start writing?

A: I did not do any creative writing until I was forty, while I was living in Africa. Years earlier, I'd been the editor of my college newspaper. One thing that experience taught me was not to value my writing so much that it couldn't be changed. In a newspaper, a whole article can be struck for lack of space. I'd also worked for the Arizona Parks Department putting out a weekly newsletter. There I had an editor who used to blue-pencil everything that was interesting in what I wrote. That was very good training too, because it taught me not to be upset when people criticized my writing.

Writing fiction came on me suddenly. When I had my son—I was living in Africa then—I gave up my job and stayed home and took care of him, which of course I wanted to do. During that time, I lost my hold on the science world, and when I wanted to go back to work, I found I couldn't get another job. I was very, very bored and felt very frustrated staying at home and talking to a little child all day. I was used to having a lot of freedom, and I wanted to get out and do something. Then one day I was reading a novel and came to a description of a frozen lake with children walking around it. Something about that description really got to me, and I went over to the typewriter and started writing a story of my own. I wrote for four hours in a trance. When I was done, I had written a short story that was not half bad, and I had realized what a wonderful feeling it was to be writing something. I found it was a way of escaping my situation. After that, I went to the typewriter and wrote every chance I got. And ever since then, I've been a writer.

Q: What was it about Shona culture that appealed to you so much?

A: There's a real system there, a sense of a world order. Nothing is ever empty in the Shona culture. The air seems full of spirits. There's the animal world and then there's the spirit world, made up of all your ancestors, so you never feel all alone out there in the bush. A lot of these people lead very lonely lives, but because of the spirit world, they're always in the middle of a community.

I like the Shona people because they like to sit down and talk a lot. You ask them a question and they will talk for hours. For this reason, it's one of the easiest cultures in the world to study. And they have all kinds of stories. But to really understand the culture, I also had to read books about it. That's how I knew what questions to ask.

Q: Did your ideas about African cultures change between the time you arrived in Africa and the time you returned to the United States?

A: I was pretty open-minded from the start. Anybody who studies psychology, as I did, knows that psychology is really pretty close to magic. I'd also studied religions, and so I also knew that religion gets into questions that science can't pin down, and that have their own validity. So when I got to Africa, it seemed reasonable to me that these people had worked out a way to live and to think that was psychologically valid for them, and I was perfectly willing to look at their culture and not judge it as a "scientist."

Q: Why in *The Ear, the Eye and the Arm* did you write about the city of Harare in the year 2194?

A: While I was living in Zimbabwe, I worked with a publishing company there on a series of books for young people called Spellbinders—books that kids would read for fun. The first thing I needed to find out was what those kids liked to read. So I went around to all the secondhand bookstores and asked what the kids were buying. They were buying science fiction, which I think appealed to them in part because it seemed connected to what they already knew about the spirit world. So I sat down to write an African science fiction story. The first book I wrote was not very

CHAPTER FOUR: AUNT GRENDELYN

"My great-aunt Grendelyn lived at the court of Queen Tyre in the Norseland," began Lorelei, moving slightly to keep from touching the cold side of the truck. "Did I tell you my family was royal?"

"Often," said Sargon, tucking his paws underneath his body for warmth.

"Tyre was a great queen, well-known for her beauty but not, I am afraid, for her goodness," said Lorelei. "You had only to mention her name in certain monasteries to the south for men to turn pale and cross themselves. Still, she was very rich. She gave rings of gold to her warriors and great banquets when they returned from battle.

"The feasts of Queen Tyre were famous. Her dragon's tail garnished with oysters was the envy of courts from Cathay to Rome, and her pickled herring -- well!"

"Please don't talk about food," said Sargon.

"Are you sure there isn't anything to eat in this miserable truck?"

"I looked a dozen times."

"Well," sighed Lorelei, "Queen Tyre's parties weren't only known for food, but entertainment. She had dwarves and clowns and the best bards to be found in Europe."

"What's a bard?" said Sargon.

"Someone who makes up stories and sings them to music. There was a small problem with the bards. They knew a certain amount of magic. It didn't do to anger one.

"Queen Tyre was having a wonderful feast in honour of pillaging an orphanage, and during it she decided to parade some of the new good because I didn't really know how to write then. I didn't know what I was doing. Later, when I wrote the American edition of *The Ear, the Eye and the Arm,* I didn't even look at that earlier version. I just wrote from scratch. So it's a different book.

Q: Resthaven, the traditional village you write about in *The Ear, the Eye and the Arm,* is a strange and fascinating place. It's sort of like a museum village or theme park.

A: Or a game preserve—but one that no outsiders are allowed to visit. It's there for the people in the story as a kind of spiritual reservoir, as a place that remains untouched by the modern world. The Masks are invaders from the outside world who have put the "spirit of the people"—the thing that keeps their culture whole—at risk. In Resthaven, it's kept safe.

Q: What did you do when you came back to live in the United States?

A: I worked in the laboratory of a mad scientist who wanted to map the DNA of fruit flies and win the Nobel Prize. He had us working on deforming fruit flies. Some of them had legs coming out of their heads or their stomachs. Some had twisted wings. My job was to keep all of these genetic strains going.

In order to do this, I would have to get them to mate. Now, fruit flies do a little dance to get into the mood. So I would take a toothpick and wiggle the male. You know, like "Hey, baby! Look at me!" I felt like a fruit fly pimp. Plus, I didn't much like having all these deformed insects around. The whole thing felt bad to me.

I put some of that feeling into *The House of the Scorpion*. People don't generally know that messing around with DNA is almost always lethal. When Dolly the sheep was cloned, I think they had around

250 failures before they got a good lamb. They had to destroy some of the rejects. What are you going to do with 250 reject babies before you get the perfect one? It was a very, very depressing job. I had taken it because we needed the money.

As for writing, any time I got a little chance, I would sit down at the typewriter. I began writing *Do You Know Me* that way, under those really awful conditions. Finally, I quit my job, and with the money I received from a National Endowment for the Arts grant, I finished *Do You Know Me*. Then I found a publisher and I began working on *The Ear, the Eye and the Arm*.

Q: Do you have a daily work routine?

A: I write whenever I get a chance. I try to write every day. I prefer doing it when I'm the only one at home. I don't answer the phone when I'm working. I discovered recently that when I write nonstop for a long time every day, the quality goes up. The writing is more intense and better. It's very tiring but it's worth it.

Q: Do you know from the start how a book will end?

A: I know the beginning and the end and I know nothing in between. I make no outline. I sit down and just let it come. I find that writing is a lot like playing the piano, which I learned as a child. I just sort of open the door to the subconscious and let it happen. I write a book in one long stream and then I cut it into chapters when I'm finished.

Q: What kinds of research do you do for your books?

A: I do painstaking research. When I wrote *A Girl Named Disaster*, I read about four hundred publications to make sure I got all the facts right. I wanted it to work not only as a novel but also as a textbook in African studies. There are fantastic elements and science fiction elements in my books, but if something is supposed to be real, then I make sure it is real—that the food is actually served in the way I describe, that the sheep are actually born at the time of year I say they are. In that regard, I follow the same rules that I did when I was a scientist. I did as much research for *The Sea of Trolls* as I did for *A Girl Named Disaster*.

Q: Do you revise your work?

A: I've gotten to the point now where the first draft is pretty close to the last draft.

Q: What do you tell young people who say they want to write?

A: The rules are pretty general. Read as much as you can and write as much as you can. I also have practical suggestions such as: Take a novel that you really like and read it three times, one time after another. Type out part of a novel you like. You can sometimes learn about writing from the physical act of writing something out. I recommend James N. Frey's *How to Write a Damn Good Novel* and Stephen King's *Danse Macabre,* which tells a lot about plot and suspense even though it's about horror movies rather than about novels. And I say not to worry about rejection slips because there are tons of editors and something will work out.

Q: What do you like best about being a writer?

A: It's a wonderful thing. It's the most fun of anything I do, and I can do it wherever I happen to be, even in the middle of the Gobi Desert. It's like living another life. You can see the whole scene. The characters become really real. You disappear into this other existence.

A NANCY FARMER READER

Do You Know Me, illustrated by Shelley Jackson (Richard
    Jackson/Orchard, 1993)

The Ear, the Eye and the Arm (Richard Jackson/Orchard, 1994)

A Girl Named Disaster (Richard Jackson/Orchard, 1996)

The House of the Scorpion (Richard Jackson/Atheneum, 2002)

The Sea of Trolls (Richard Jackson/Atheneum, 2004)

The Warm Place (Richard Jackson/Orchard, 1995)

BRIAN JACQUES

Born 1939, Liverpool, England

B RIAN JACQUES is a wiry, restless, irrepressibly talkative man with a gravelly voice that seems the perfect match for the piratical glint in his eye. A natural performer, Jacques says that the Redwall character he feels closest to is Gonff, the agile "mousethief" who while scavenging to ensure his own survival makes a point of helping others.

Jacques grew up in poverty, went to sea at the age of fifteen, and later worked as a railway fireman, longshoreman, policeman, and milk deliveryman. A lifelong resident of Liverpool, he was performing comic monologues in the city's nightclubs when a new rock band called the Beatles was also just coming along. Twenty years later, by then the host of a popular radio program, Jacques volunteered to read to the children at Liverpool's Royal Wavertree School for the Blind. He decided to try his own hand at writing for children after coming across shelfloads of "realistic" novels that struck him as needlessly grim. The happy result of his initial after-hours effort was *Redwall* (1986). Published when Jacques was already in his late forties, *Redwall* marked the start of yet another new career for its author and of a multigenerational saga now known to readers throughout the world.

In stories in which the moral battle lines are always clearly drawn, Redwall's creator takes pride in making his "baddies" as "interesting" as his more admirable characters. As for the heroes, Jacques says with old-fashioned conviction, "My values are not based on violence . . . [but] on courage. . . . A warrior isn't somebody like Bruce Willis or Arnold Schwarzenegger. A warrior can be any age."

Leonard S. Marcus: What kind of child were you?

Brian Jacques: I was a swine! A good swimmer. A good boxer. A good singer. I could tell stories. I always had good handwriting. I had it caned into me by the Little Sisters of the Screaming Skull!

No kid ever thought I was an egghead. It didn't do to be an egghead in the neighborhood I lived in. Some of the kids used to have fun just beating up college kids in uniforms if they caught them going through the neighborhood. We used to say, "The cat with a tail is a tourist." I could handle myself. I was Jack the Lad!

I used to do a job after school from the time I was eleven years old. I wouldn't be relying on me own father for pocket money. He wouldn't give you the push off the pavement. So I was self-sufficient, and I enjoyed meself. I hated school, but I enjoyed meself. I just wanted to get out of school and get to sea.

Q: Do you remember World War II?

A: Liverpool was a big seaport, and we were living right by the docks. Up until I was five or six, the Germans bombed the hell out of us every night, and I remember that vividly. Because our family was so poor, our only escape was the movies, the palace of dreams.

Q: What kinds of movies did you see?

A: It was through the movies I saw when I was a kid that America to me became the magic land—Oz. Unlike my poor family, Americans had everything: iceboxes, big cars, nice houses. Cowboys lived there. I still have that feeling when I come to America. It's still a place of wonder to me.

Q: What else do you remember about the war?

A: I remember the shortages and being hungry as a kid. That was how all the food found its way into my books. I never saw milk chocolate or tasted a banana until I was six years old. I hated the banana and spit it out. It tasted so rich and so foreign. Sometimes during the war my mother's sister who lived next door would get out her cookbooks, and we'd look at the illustrations: peach melba gâteau, devil's food chocolate cake! It really irritated me when I would read in some storybook, "The king gave the four friends a great feast, after which they rode off on their white horses . . ." I'd think, Just a minute! What did the feast look like? What did it taste like? Was there plenty for everybody? So I tell about all that in the Redwall books.

Q: What did you read as a child?

A: Most of the books I read came either from discovering them meself

Brian Jacques (middle), with brothers, circa 1949

or from my old man, who was a very strict man and would just hand me a book once in a while. He'd always say, "That's a good yarn."

My first great book I discovered myself. I was about ten, and I was down at the back of the old St. John's Market, in Liverpool, in a big old secondhand bookshop. I used to go in and look around at all these dusty old volumes. They had library ladders on rollers, and you could pull yourself along the top shelf. On that particular day, I found a tattered, Morocco-bound copy of Homer's *Iliad* and *Odyssey*. It was seven shilling and sixpence, which to me then was a fortune. So I turned the book around and put it back on the shelf so nobody else would see it. It was about a week before I got that seven shilling and sixpence and went down and bought it. Some of the lines in that book! The power of the writing. "'Who is that warrior, who strides like a sheep among wolves?' 'Sire, that is Odysseus, whom some call Ulysses.'" You got the picture of these great powerful Greek warriors. My book had been given in 1864 as a present to a twelve-year-old girl—there was a little sticker inside—called Sarah Holmes, at the Merchant Tailors' School for Girls, for having won first prize in literature. I kept that book till it fell to bits.

Q: It seems you learned a lot from it.

A: I attended the university of life. I went off to sea when I was fifteen. In England you went to an elementary school until you were fifteen, and if your parents didn't have the money to send you further, you got a job to put some money on the table to help with the family. I was no raving intellectual, musing about the dreaming spires of Oxford. I wanted to go to sea, like all my uncles in the Merchant Marine—all happily drunk in a secondhand suit from New York and looking like they were somebody!

Q: Did you like school?

A: I started at St. John's, which was a boys' school with fifty-two boys in a class, when I was ten. I call it St. John's School for the Totally Bewildered. I can remember my first teacher there to this day. He was a physically small man but very vicious. Spoke very little—and caned a lot. On the first day he gave us assessment tests and had us write a one-page essay on "the peculiarities of animals." He said, "You know: a dog that rolls over and does dead or a pussycat that can open the door with his paw." I remembered reading a "Ripley's Believe It or Not" column in the *Sunday Express* about a bird that cleaned a crocodile's teeth, without getting eaten by the crocodile. So I wrote a page about that. Our papers were collected and later, as we were doing the next task, suddenly the teacher called out, "JACK-QUEZ!" People were always mispronouncing my name. "Jakes, sir," I said. "Come here!" he said. "The rest of you get on with your work."

So I had to come and stand alongside his desk, and then he said, "Where did you copy this?" I said, "I didn't copy it, sir. I wrote it." "How old are you, Mr. Jacques?" I said, "Ten, sir." "Well, let me tell you something. Boys of ten do not write like this! If you continue to stand there and lie to me, I shall cane you. But if you admit you copied it, you can go and sit down." I stuck to me guns. So he said, "Hold up your hand." Afterwards, I thought, I can *write*—and he don't know it!

I still go down to St. John's to see Father Godfrey Kearny, who is ninety-four now. I knock on the door and say, "Godfrey. Haven't you been sent to go back to headquarters yet?" He answers, "Oh, Brian Jacques, you sinful man. Come in, come in!"

Q: Were there storytellers in your family?

A: My old granddad, who died when I was eleven, had been to sea all his life. When he used to come to my house, mom would say, "Da's up," and she'd make him sandwiches and a cup of tea, and he'd take me to the park and sit and talk to me about the time he got yellow fever and the time he got stuck to the deck in the Tropics by the tar. He'd fallen asleep while he was drunk and the tar melted under him. He'd tell about robbing heathen temples. Oh, he was a good owl, a good yarner.

Q: How did you become a writer?

A: I first started out writing in the late 1950s, early '60s. My brothers and I used to go to folk clubs, and I seen so many people gettin' up and doin' their own compositions. My two brothers said to me, "You can do better than that!" Being Jack the Lad, I thought, Of course! So I started to write comic monologues. I even rewrote the

Bible in Liverpool street slang, which is called Scouse. I performed my monologues in clubs: "Now the Lord made the mush called Adam, and he said, 'There you are now, lad. You're the very first fella to be on earth.' And Adam said: 'But who's me dad?' 'Don't ask awkward questions,' said God. 'You're alive, you're well, and breathing. I've arranged to put you in this park.' He called it the Garden of Eden."

I done them on television. I had seven books of my monologues published early on. I was also working as a longshoreman then, and I wrote lots of stories and songs about the conditions of the workers and about the way the city planners were destroying Liverpool by putting up so many high-rise flats: "Towering over church and steeple / Are filing cabinets for people."

I was also broadcasting for BBC Liverpool and beginning to make a few bucks, and so I adopted the children of the Royal School for the Blind in Liverpool and got an appeal going that has raised lots and lots of money over the years. I used to go and play with the kids and read them stories. With the younger kids I'd say, "What story are you going to have?" They'd say, "Little Red Riding Hood"! . . . and I'd think, Oh, God, I've read it to them sixty times. So, to make it more interesting, I would start: "Twice upon a time . . ." And they'd go, *"Once!"* Then I'd say, "Oh, sorry. . . . There was a little boy . . ." *"Girl!"* "Whose name was Blue Riding Hood . . ." *"Red!"*

With the older kids, I would read the new books that were being sent in by publishers and well-meaning people, and I found that I didn't like what I read. They were all basically books about this mess we're living in the middle of called modern-day life: teenage angst

Once in a time long gone of golden dew dropped mornings, high sunny afternoons, and crimson pink twilights, the green depths that men and animals knew as Mossflower woods lay as it had been since time out of mind. There at the south border half shaded by mighty trees on one side and open to the green sward on the other was Redwall Abbey, from above it looked like a great dusty jewel fallen between a cloth of light and dark green velvet. The good monks had built Redwall from the red sandstone which they quarried from local pits, all over the south face the venerable building was practically overgrown with the species of ivy known as Virginia creeper, which in late autumn turned its leaves a most brilliant red adding further glory to the name of Redwall Abbey.

However, it was June now and little Matthias as he crossed the cloisters happily flip flopping his sandals with the tip of his tail peeping from beneath his dark green novices habit looked up at the shiny green ivy leaves, as he did so he tripped and went

Draft page for the prologue to *Redwall*

and divorce problems and abuse. I thought, Where's the magic? The good yarns and adventures? So I wrote *Redwall*.

I bought myself a packet of pens and a load of cheap recycled pads. I wrote every night after I'd come in from the clubs. I'd sit up most of the night, with the dog looking at me as if I was stupid. You know, When are you going to bed? It turned out to be eight hundred pages of this thick recycled paper. I kept it in a plastic Safeway supermarket shopping bag. I was on my way to the School for the Blind one day and stopped in at the Everyman Theatre, where I'd been the writer in residence. The man who was chairman of the theatre at the time, a dapper little man named Allen Durband, always wanted to read anything that I wrote. He would say to me, "I know you can write, but you're too much of a bloody rough diamond!" I was a folksinger, a standup comic, a newspaper columnist, the whole lot. "You're spread too bloody wide, Brian." So on this day, when he asked me, "Now tell me, Brian, what have you been writing?" I said, "It's a kids' story. Your time is far too valuable to read it." But Allen said, "No, no. If you've written it, I want to read it." So I gave him my only copy of *Redwall* and thought no more of it. I didn't hear from him for four months. Finally when I saw him, I said, "Did you ever read it?" "Do you know what I've done with it?" he said. "I sent it to my publishers with a note saying they'd be fools if they didn't publish it." So, that was it.

Q: Have the other jobs you've had helped you as a writer?

A: Oh yeah. When you go to sea, or you're a cop, or a long-distance truck driver, or you deliver milk—all of which I did at one time or another—you see people with all their frailties and their strengths. You make friends and meet people you'd never think would be in them jobs. You talk to people and see life through their eyes as well as your own. All things you couldn't get from books.

Q: Do you have a daily work routine?

A: I don't really. I have a mercurial temperament. I do write every day but not to the destruction of everything. I get up. I go for a swim back in me old neighborhood. I come home, have a bite to eat, have a talk with the dog, sit down, write, and when I feel I've written enough, get up. I seldom do more than ten pages a day now, although I know I can do twenty-five on a good day.

Q: Ten is a lot, don't you think?

A: Nah! I'm very fortunate in that once I have an idea for a book and it gets going, I can take it to bed with me every night, and I can further it, and further it, and further it. The next morning when I sit at the typewriter, I know exactly what I'm going to do.

Q: Tell me about your dog.

A: Ah, Teddy! I've always had a West Highland white terrier. They like being close to people, but they're a brave little dog. You can imagine that if they could speak, they would have a Scottish accent: "Aye, like *this,* Jimmy! Aye!" They are very, very faithful little dogs.

If I have an idea for a book, I go down to the old neighborhood with Teddy and walk around Stanley Park, which was the countryside of my childhood, living in the inner city. I can still see Stanley Park as I saw it when I was a kid. The boating lake is a vast ocean. The sports field is an endless desert. The little clump of trees is a vast primeval forest. There's a whole world there. I still see that, and I still have that lovely feeling. The big red sandstone wall lies along the back of the bowling green, with the green door that's been rusted shut with the years. What's on the other side? I know now what's on the other side, this little soccer ground. But I still have that sense of magic.

Q: So, the red wall is . . . Redwall?

A: Yeah.

Q: Do you know from the start how a book will end?

A: You always start off thinking you have an outline. You start off with one idea and one character, and then somehow or other within three chapters you're jugglin' fifteen balls in the air. Eventually I'll reach the goal—but by such devious ways!

Q: Do you revise your work?

A: When I finish a page, I'll look at it and I'll go, The word *and* occurs too much in this. Me two enemies in life are *and* and *the*. If I can substitute other words or punctuation for either, it makes it flow so much better.

Q: Do you ever base your characters on real people?

A: One of my greatest fans is a Queen's counsel [a kind of lawyer] in Liverpool, Sir Harry Livermore. He's eighty-two, and we go swimming together. He said to me one day, "Brian, I want to be in your books, you know." So I said, "Is that right, Sir Harry? What would you like to be?" "I'd like to be a rat!" I said, "You've been a rat long enough. You can be an owl." So I put him in *Mattimeo* as an owl called Sir Harry the Muse, who "spoke in rhyme all the time, / except when it was business."

Q: What do children tell you about your books?

A: One thing the kids will sometimes say is, "Someone got killed, one of the good guys!" I say, "Well, it happens—because there is both life and death. At some point you are going to lose someone close to you, maybe your granddad or your grandma. But the lesson is this:

If it's a loved one you've lost, you haven't lost them. He or she is still there in your memory."

Q: What do you tell children who want to write?

A: I tell them to learn to paint pictures with words. When I write, I see the pictures in my mind. It's very vivid to me. I was talking to a scriptwriter for television once, and he said that for him the best thing is to imagine sitting in your favorite armchair at home and switching on the television. Then imagine what you would want to come up on that screen. That's what you write.

Q: What do you like best about being a writer?

A: Well, there are a few things. They say that fame is fleeting. But the nice thing about writing is that writing is always *there*. When I'm gone, my books will still be on the shelves. Also, it's nice to know that the more books you write, and the better they become, and the more your readers like them, the more respect you get. And I'll never have to drive another truck again!

My father and mother would be shocked to death to see me now. My father said when I was at school, "What do you want to be when you leave school, boy?" "I want to be an author, sir." He said, "Don't be so stupid! Go and sit down!" Authors to him were dead people with names like Sir Arthur Conan Doyle. I still have dreams now and then of being out of work and looking round trying to get back into jobs I'd done in the past. It takes a lot of getting used to.

I love it that as a writer you work with the poetry and music of words. Words are as wild as rocky peaks. They're as smooth as a millpond and as sunny as a day in a meadow. Words are beautiful things. Every word matters.

A BRIAN JACQUES READER

The Redwall series:

Redwall (Philomel, 1986)

Mossflower (Philomel, 1988)

Mattimeo (Philomel, 1990)

Mariel of Redwall (Philomel, 1992)

Salamandastron (Philomel, 1993)

Martin the Warrior (Philomel, 1994)

The Bellmaker (Philomel, 1995)

Outcast of Redwall (Philomel, 1996)

Pearls of Lutra (Philomel, 1997)

The Long Patrol (Philomel, 1998)

Marlfox (Philomel, 1998)

The Legend of Luke (Philomel, 2000)

Lord Brocktree (Philomel, 2000)

Taggerung (Philomel, 2001)

Triss (Philomel, 2002)

Loamhedge (Philomel, 2003)

Rakkety Tam (Philomel, 2004)

High Rhulain (Philomel, 2005)

DIANA WYNNE JONES

Born 1934, London, England

D IANA WYNNE JONES grew up at a time when schoolchildren were routinely punished for writing left-handed
and dyslexia was mistaken for a sign of below-average in-
telligence. Being both left-handed *and* dyslexic might well have
warned off another young person from a writing career. But in Jones's
case, the urge to tell stories, bolstered by a bred-in-the-bone habit of
defiance, somehow won out anyway. Jones's early difficulties eventually even served her, as material for tough-minded, strange, and
wildly irreverent fantasies in which a castle can suddenly become air-
borne, a heavenly "luminary" can be sentenced to roam the earth as
a dog, and nothing in reality ever proves to be reliably solid.

Growing up during World War II in the care of overbusy, not
especially child-friendly parents also had a lot to do with the kind of
writer she has become. So, too, has the comparatively quiet, steady

life Jones has since led as the wife of a university professor, the mother of three children, and an author with schools to visit and publishers' deadlines to meet. As one commentator has poignantly observed, "Her husband and sons taught her what a normal family life was like, and she began to understand how abnormal her own childhood had been." Perhaps one reason she writes so often about characters who shuttle between worlds is that, in doing so, she is simply describing a version of her own experience. Jones herself says that she considers each new book an "experiment," an attempt to "write the ideal book, the book my children would like, the book I *didn't* have as a child myself."

Leonard S. Marcus: What kind of child were you?

Diana Wynne Jones: I was quite stroppy and contrary, I think. I would hate to have taught myself at school. I was always the one who spotted the flaw in the argument and asked the awkward question. I was the oldest of three, so I tended to be rather bossy—very bossy at times, because my sisters are bossy themselves. I had to have the biggest war ax.

I liked nothing more than to rush about laughing and having adventures. If I didn't have adventures, I made some up to have. I must have looked an absolute freak, too, because among the other things that we didn't get when I was a child was any clothing. We all wore castoffs from charity homes. I must have been a very weird object.

Q: There was a woman living in the neighborhood where I grew up named Mrs. Charmer, whom my friends and I all thought was a witch. Did you know anyone like that as a child?

A: Oh indeed, yes. In fact I put the very woman in *Witch's Business*. She was just asking for it, really. She was probably mad and eccentric, but I always thought she *could* have been a witch. She lived all alone in a crazy little cottage. She was hideous as sin and wore thick pebble glasses and walked in a curious stooping, rushing way, rather like an emu. And she wore most peculiar clothing that she picked up anywhere and had her hair in skinny pigtails. The village kids one and all were convinced she was a witch, though as far I know there was no proof of it.

There were also, in Thaxted, two other ladies who frankly avowed that they were witches. They belonged to the same family, and you went to one for the bad things and the other for the good things.

Q: Were there storytellers in your family?

A: My grandfather was a famous preacher. He was a mesmerizer! Because he spoke only in Welsh, I couldn't understand a word, but I always imagined that listening to him was like listening to the prophet Elijah.

Q: Has your grandfather appeared as a character in any of your books?

A: No, because he was totally unapproachable. If you are going to write about someone you need to have been able to "walk round them," to see them from a certain distance. I never could with my grandfather because he was always such a gigantic figure to me.

Q: Did you model the sisters in *Howl's Moving Castle* on yourself and your own two younger sisters?

A: A little bit, yes. It was kind of difficult for me, being the eldest, as it is in *Howl's Moving Castle* for Sophie, because as the eldest you were the one who wasn't going to succeed, whereas the youngest child obviously was. My middle sister was very beautiful, so I suppose that gave rise to Lettie.

Q: As a child you crossed paths with two famous children's book authors, Arthur Ransome and Beatrix Potter. Would you tell about those experiences?

A: I didn't myself actually meet Beatrix Potter. What happened was that one of my sisters and another little girl of the same age were on a walk with me. It was a very long walk, and at one point they went on ahead. Eventually, they became tired and found this beautiful farm gate on which they hooked their heels and rested their elbows and swung, which was restful. My memory is of them running back toward where I was, crying their eyes out and saying this horrible old woman with a sack over her head had come and hit them for swinging on her gate. And that, as it turned out, was Beatrix Potter!

The encounter with Arthur Ransome was similarly unfortunate. We were living in a kind of colony of mothers and children who had been evacuated during the war. One of the mothers had taken all the younger children to play on a pebbly beach by the lake, in the same bay where there was a houseboat. They weren't particularly obstreperous or anything. They were just playing when a man came rowing over in a small dinghy and told them off for disturbing him. He announced his intention to come over to where we were living to complain, which he did the next day. The mothers in the meantime had all run around and found rare things for him—things like coffee and biscuits that were hard to obtain during the war—but he didn't stay for any of them. He stayed only about five minutes—and it was then that I saw the great Arthur Ransome.

I was five years old at the time and had just gotten into trouble for refusing to learn to sew. I was being taught by one of the mothers, who had this very old-fashioned idea that girls *should* learn to sew. The boys were doing something quite different and much more interesting. I had said I wasn't going to learn. I announced that I was too young! Finally, when asked if I didn't want to grow up to be a lady, I said, no, I didn't! Then I put my tongue out at her. This was the last straw, so I was dumped into the hall in punishment. And that is why I happened to be there when Arthur Ransome swept by.

He was quite small and chubby and had a beard, which was fairly unusual in those days. What it makes you realize is that people who write books are real people you can come within touching distance of and that some people who write enchanting books are not enchanting people at all.

Q: Did growing up during World War II affect you as a writer?

A: Yes, because from the time I was five years old until the time I was getting on to twelve, the entirety of the world as far as I was concerned was stark-staring crazy in a most menacing way. It left me with the feeling that the most appalling and peculiar things are liable to happen at any time. Later, I came to think that if only people then had read a little more fantasy, they would have known Hitler for a dark lord.

Also, all the adults that one came into contact with then, without exception, were behaving like children. Like children, they were much more liable to burst into tears, for example, and cry for an hour for something very simple. Everyone was under such stress.

I've always felt that there really is no difference between adults and children, and I think this is probably why.

Q: It sounds as if you think of fantasy writing as "true to life" and not the opposite, as some people would say.

A: Absolutely. This has been reinforced by the tendency of all my books to come true. There are bizarre episodes that I think I've made up, and then a year or so later those very things happen to me. *Witch Week,* for instance, takes place in a boarding school at Halloween. It was just published when I found I had to spend the week of Halloween at a very old-fashioned boarding school. There's an episode in the book in which one of the girls finds it impossible to stop describing the food, which is perfectly atrocious, to the headmistress, whom she's sitting beside on the high table. At this meal, they have a starter that is supposed to be prawn cocktail, but the girl just looks at it and says it's "worms in custard." During my school visit, we had a grand dinner in a huge Gothic hall, and when I looked down at the first course I was served, I thought, My goodness, this *is* worms in custard!

But the most striking example is *Drowned Ammet,* which is one of the Dalemark quartet. The story more or less ends with an island rising up magically out of the sea and breaking a huge sailing ship in two, then greening over, growing grass and so forth, in an incredibly short time. There's also an element of terrorism: the hero tries to plant a bomb in a procession. This came true when somebody asked me to christen a boat. I was terribly flattered to have been asked, and then there I was with these enthusiastic, nice people and their boat, which was most fortunately a catamaran, so it was in two pieces already. They handed me two little bottles of airline champagne and said,

"Would you pour one—don't break it, please!—over each of the hulls and would you please invoke the gods?" I asked them if they were sure they didn't want me to break the bottles. Boat builders had told me that it was terribly bad luck if you *didn't* break the bottles. I asked them twice and they still said they were sure.

So I did as they asked, and then we all got onto the boat and started sailing. We sailed for about five minutes—it really wasn't very long—before an island came up out of the sea covered with grass, and we found we were completely stranded, miles from anywhere, sitting on top of this trickling grassy mound, with acres of sea all around. We finally ended up knee deep in mud, floundering onto shore, where-upon we were politely arrested by some very superior soldiers because we had accidentally landed in a military training area. They thought we might be terrorists! I thought, Oh my goodness, all the elements of this book are coming together. I did however catch my train home.

Q: When did you start writing?

A: I started when I was eight years old. I was at that point highly dyslexic and had trouble writing two or three sentences let alone a whole book.

It was the middle of the afternoon, and I had been sent away to rest. Looking back on it, my parents really did not like children! They got rid of us on all sorts of pretexts. So I was sort of sitting there, very obediently, on my bed, having been told I needed a rest, and it was as if somebody suddenly came along and touched me on the shoul-der and said, "Excuse me. You're going to be a writer. Did you know that?" It was an utter and total conviction, which I later went and told my parents about. They laughed of course, because I really did have

difficulties. But from then on, I did write and with practice it got easier.
I think I read *Alice's Adventures in Wonderland* round that same time.

Then when we moved to Thaxted, where there were no books at
all, I started writing so that I would have something to read aloud to
my sisters. In that way I managed to finish two extremely bad books.
But I finished them. *Rolling Rory* was about a boy on roller skates who
had all kinds of weird and wonderful adventures. It filled twelve
exercise books. My other book, which was even longer, was about a
gang of child detectives and was called *Sandy Investigates*. Writing these
two bad books was a good experience in a way, as I knew then that
I was capable of writing something "full-length."

**Q: When did you first realize that you had an unusual, near "photographic"
memory?**

A: When I was at school, the very first time I did an exam. I would
close my eyes and simply "read" the page of notes. It was particularly
useful in the case of geography, because the geography master did
nothing but dictate notes. He never *taught*. So everything was in the
notes. It was perfect!

Q: Did your special memory feel like a magical power to you?

A: Memory does seem like magic, doesn't it? In *Fire and Hemlock*, the heroine, Polly, has a whole set of what turn out to be completely false memories. The magic is hidden away behind those false memories. It's very easy to convince yourself of an untruth. Disentangling that, and discovering the real truth, is quite a magical process.

Q: As a college student, you went to hear J. R. R. Tolkien lecture. What was he like?

A: I went to his public lectures. They were absolutely appalling. In those days a lecturer could be paid for his entire course even if he lost his audience, provided he turned up for the first lecture. I think that Tolkien made quite a cynical effort to get rid of us so he could go home and finish writing *Lord of the Rings*. He gave his lectures in a very, very small room and didn't address us, his audience, at all. In fact he looked the other way, with his face almost squashed up against the blackboard. He spoke in a mutter. His mind was on finishing *Lord of the Rings,* and he was really musing to himself about the nature of narrative. But I found this so fascinating that I came back week after week, as did one other person. I've always wondered what became of him, because he was obviously equally fascinated. And because we stuck there, Tolkien couldn't go away and write *Lord of the Rings!* He would say the most marvelous things about the way you take a very basic plot and twitch it here and twitch it there—and it becomes a completely different plot.

Q: Why do you think fantasy is so much more popular now than it was when you were growing up, or when Tolkien was writing?

A: The two world wars were the worst kind of madness. Fantasy helps you think more clearly when things are mad. Fantasy is actually helpful. But whether it's because people have finally realized this now, I don't know. It may just be one of those unexplained things.

Q: C. S. Lewis was also at Oxford when you were a student there, wasn't he?

A: Yes. He was completely the opposite from Tolkien. He had a great, deep, rolling voice and lectured in the very biggest of the lecture halls because he was intensely popular. *He* was mesmerizing. He and my grandfather would have gotten along like a house on fire! Lewis would talk about the Middle Ages—often about small, queer details of that time that in the hands of other people would have been extremely boring. He would walk up and down—this rolling, little pear shape— tolling out in his great deep voice. You just hung on his words.

Q: *Howl's Moving Castle* is dedicated to a boy who, you say, asked during a school visit that you write a book about a moving castle. Was that suggestion all you needed to get started?

A: It was about eighteen months later that I realized that a moving castle was a marvelous idea and I needed to write a book about it.

The origins of books are very strange. At least two of mine have started with a picture. *Fire and Hemlock* started with a photograph that is also called "Fire and Hemlock." A photograph by Eliot Porter called "Intimate Landscape" gave rise to *Hexwood*. It's a picture of a wood which you can't see the end of. I have it hanging right by the telephone at home.

Dogsbody was inspired by our Labrador, who was an extremely intelligent dog and a fully paid-up member of the family. My mother-in-law was coming to stay with us in a cottage in the country. She was one of those people who, without ever actually saying it, demands two kinds of cake and three kinds of sandwiches the moment she arrives, all perfectly done. I was trying to do all this, and it was pouring rain outside, when my dog came in. He just hated to be wet, which for a Labrador—a marsh dog and a retriever—is absurd. But he hated it! He came in soaking wet, and although I was extremely preoccupied, he managed all the same to make it clear to me not only that he was miserable but that he needed a towel—now. He actually took me to the towel cupboard and more or less batted at the door. As he did this, I thought, This is amazingly clever! And then I thought it must be perfectly appalling to be that clever in a dog's body. My mother-in-law never got her tea because I went away and immediately tried to write chapter one!

Q: Do you have a daily work routine?

A: I wish I did! I can't do it like that at all. I have to wait until enough of a book has gathered. Sometimes I just sit still, and stare outside, and wait.

If you're lucky, you get the initial idea, and then it gathers to itself large swathes of the rest of what is going to happen. You can almost feel it slide into your head in lumps. When you've got enough present, you can start writing. Once the book is coming through fast, I forget to eat and stay up all night.

Q: Do you know from the start how a book will end?

A: I always know the beginning and a lot about the people in it and their various likes and motives. And I'll know very clearly a scene from the middle. I'll have it all in full color in my head. Very often I know the end, too, though that isn't always the case.

Q: Have you ever written a book with a series in mind?

A: Never. Each book has just happened along. I'll have a sudden feeling that, My goodness, there is this book sort of bulging out of the side of one I wrote two or three years earlier. My books rarely are direct sequels but just sort of hook in somewhere in the middle.

Q: How do you know when a book is done?

A: That's not a problem for me. Sometimes an editor will ask me to tie up a few more loose ends. But I'm in favor of a book that leaves one or two unanswered questions for readers to nibble away at.

Q: Do you revise your work?

A: Yes, I do. In order to get the story flowing properly, I don't stop and pick up discrepancies until the second draft. I do an immensely careful second draft. I take ages and ages and ages, making sure that everything fits in that possibly can.

Q: Do you do research for your books?

A: Not specifically for a book. I find that stops me dead. I just generally read and think about mythology and archeology, astronomy and physics: the huge and fantastic things. Not that I can understand physics terribly well! I let my reading simmer down in the bottom of my brain, where it turns into something else. I made up the word *chrestomancy*. Then I found out it actually means "useful knowledge" in Greek.

Q: What do you tell children who want to write?

A: A lot of children these days believe you need a license to write, so you have to tell them that that isn't so! I tell them that writing a book is like reading one, only slower. And I say don't try and write something you're not interested in.

Q: What do you like best about being a writer?

A: One of the things is doing what I like more than anything else in the world, and being allowed to do it, and being paid to do it. It's great. And I like setting something going and seeing that all the characters are suddenly people who behave like themselves, as if they had nothing to do with me at all. They come out with remarks that I never would have thought of myself personally. It's a very odd feeling. I like that very much.

A DIANA WYNNE JONES READER

The Chronicles of Chrestomanci:

Charmed Life (Greenwillow, 1977)

The Magicians of Caprona (Greenwillow, 1980)

Witch Week (Greenwillow, 1982)

The Lives of Christopher Chant (Greenwillow, 1988)

Mixed Magics: Four Tales of Chrestomanci (Greenwillow, 2001)

Conrad's Fate (Greenwillow, 2005)

The Dalemark quartet:

Cart and Cwidder (Atheneum, 1977)

Drowned Ammet (Atheneum, 1978)

The Spellcoats (Atheneum, 1979)

The Crown of Dalemark (Greenwillow, 1995)

Dogsbody (Greenwillow, 1977)

Fire and Hemlock (Greenwillow, 1985)

Hexwood (Greenwillow, 1994)

Howl's Moving Castle (Greenwillow, 1986)

Witch's Business (Dutton, 1974)

URSULA K. LE GUIN

Born 1929, Berkeley, California

K NOWING NAMES," says the wizard Sparrowhawk in Ursula K. Le Guin's *The Tombs of Atuan*, "is my job. My art. To weave the magic of a thing, you see, one must find its true name out."

Le Guin grew up in a home where books and the names of things mattered. Her father, Alfred Kroeber, was one of America's pioneering anthropologists. Her mother, Theodora Kroeber, was an author whose best-known work, *Ishi in Two Worlds* (1961), was based on her husband's studies of the life of the last surviving member of the Yahi Native American tribe.

Wordstruck from childhood, Le Guin has published an amazing variety of writings including poetry, fantasy, science fiction, realistic fiction, and essays. *A Wizard of Earthsea* (1968) was her first work to be published especially for young readers, although, in characteristic fashion, that book and its sequels have defied categorization and gone on to find great numbers of devoted readers both young and old.

Written with intense clarity and lyricism, and a salty wit, the Earthsea books abound in memorable observations, descriptions, and phrases, as this small sampling, chosen almost at random, will show:

"The question is always the same, with a dragon: will he talk with you or will he eat you?" (*The Tombs of Atuan*)

"That remarkable art, walking . . ." (*Tehanu*)

"To be one's self is a rare thing, and a great one." (*The Farthest Shore*)

Leonard S. Marcus: What kind of child were you?

Ursula K. Le Guin: I was the fourth, and only girl, and welcomed as such by parents and brothers. Rather fragile as a baby, then became quite solid. Obedient, bright, a good girl. Too shy to play or talk with anyone at school until about fifth grade, when I made a couple of friends. My parents and brothers were spirited, kindly, loving, highly intelligent people; my microcosm was a sweet one.

Q: What are some of your first memories of stories and storytelling?

A: Listening to my mother read *The Swiss Family Robinson* to my older brothers and trying hard to stay awake. Listening to my great-aunt Betsy talk about her life in Wyoming and Colorado and tell stories about the family while she ironed or cooked and I hung around. Listening to my father tell northern Californian Indian stories at the campfire on summer nights in the Napa Valley. I think he was

Ursula Kroeber, age three or four, in her brother's baseball uniform

mentally translating some of them as he told them. The telling voice was very quiet and a little hesitant. Listening through the wall between our rooms to my brother Karl telling himself heroic sagas of his own invention, with a lot of bangs and "Take that!"s in them. Acting out scenes from books with my brothers. I was one of the Belgae attacking Caesar's camp (on a hill in California), about ten years before I ever read Caesar. . . . We got into a little trouble because of the catapult we built, which hurled large rocks quite efficiently. Later on, Karl was Robin Hood and I was Little John . . . "Have at thee, varlet!" We got into a little trouble because of the quarterstaff combats. As my father pointed out, a quarterstaff can be a deadly weapon—though not often when wielded by nine-year-olds.

Q: Did your parents encourage you to write? How and when did you begin?

A: My parents both read all the time, my father wrote all the time (when he wasn't teaching), and the house was full of books; reading and writing were constant, natural activities and pleasures, pretty much like eating and breathing. I started making poems quite young, at five I suppose, when I learned to write, and went on doing so. I started trying to write stories at nine or ten. I filled tiny notebooks with beginnings and sketches of stories. I submitted my first story to a magazine when I was eleven or twelve.

My parents neither specifically encouraged nor discouraged me in any way from writing poetry and stories. When I showed my writings to my parents, they made no fuss over them, did not highly praise them, but approved them fully—so that I always felt not that I was somebody special but that what I was trying to do was absolutely worth doing.

As I try to understand why their influence was so benign, it seems to me that they, my father particularly, were very much work oriented, but not particularly achievement oriented. That takes the curse off the work. "Success" is not the point. I think my father felt that to be able to do work you want to do was one of the greatest privileges and rewards life can offer. It is actually a rather rare privilege pale in the comet's glow, a horse and rider galloped, straight and level as the wide way they pounded on.

They covered twenty miles together, starting in the very deepest cold of the red night. The rider was hunched low on the big horse's neck, and saw little except the endless road and the black mane that sometimes whipped his face.

A dim light shone out in the pale dawn. The rider pulled the horse to a shuddering halt in front of a small stone hut. ~~He stopped~~. He called out, easing himself in the saddle. A

(33)

in our society. He enjoyed his work with gusto, not only his long intellectual career and his fieldwork, but also gardening and tree planting and—"whatsoever thy hand findeth to do, do it with all thy strength, and all thy heart"—have I got that right?

Q: Was there a librarian or teacher or other adult outside your family who was important to you as a young reader and writer?

A: I had good teachers in the Berkeley schools but was too shy and introverted to let them befriend me. Josephine Miles, a poet who taught at UC Berkeley, was most gentle and encouraging to me when my mother encouraged me to show her some of my poems at about age fourteen. She was a great, beloved teacher of poetry. She took me seriously and so helped me take my writing seriously.

Q: Was there a moment when you realized you were no longer a child?

A: At sixteen, seventeen, eighteen years old I worked hard at figuring out my personal responsibility for what I did with my highly privileged life and realized that this moral responsibility was also political (the fall of Czechoslovakia to the Russians was an awakening moment for me), and I guess I felt that to undertake such responsibilities was to be grownup—a burden, an honor.

Q: Do you remember when you first read J. R. R. Tolkien's *The Lord of the Rings* and what you thought of it?

A: In the mid-fifties. I had been resisting the books with their red-and-black staring-eye covers and the fulsome reviews in the *Saturday Review*. I was suspicious. But one day at the Emory University library, having nothing to read, I picked up the first volume and took it home. Next day I hurried to the library in terrible fear that somebody might have checked out the other two volumes. I got them, and my memory is that I read them in three days, which really is not pos-sible, even for careless galloping readers like me, is it? Anyhow, there-after, Middle Earth has been one of the great kingdoms of this world to me, and I have gone back and back to it, as often as to *War and Peace,* I suppose. I am grateful that I was in my twenties when I first read Tolkien and had gone far enough towards finding my own voice and way as a writer that I could learn from him (endlessly) without being overwhelmed, overinfluenced by him.

Q: The sea is such a powerful image in the Earthsea books. What do you think about when you look out at the ocean?

A: Well, one thing I think, or rather feel because it's not thinking, is that to look out westward to the ocean is natural, expectable—because I grew up looking straight out through the Golden Gate. From this I derived a deep conviction that the sea is supposed to be (a) nearby, and (b) to the west. When it's not, like in Ohio, or on the East Coast, I feel that something is wrong and ought to be attended to. (One of the immediate affinities I felt for *The Lord of the Rings* was that the ocean was in the right place.) We now have a cottage in a seaside vil-lage in Oregon; I can see a bit of the breakers from the upstairs window. I walk a half block to the dunes from which one looks north to the headlands, miles south down the great beach, and straight west to the sunset—

> *Out of the golden remote wild west where the sea without shore is,*
> *Full of the sunset, and sad, if at all, with the fullness of joy . . .*

I remember my father reading those Swinburne lines aloud and how my heart leaped at the sound and the vision and craved more. . . .

"Good," said the boy, for he had no wish to tell the secret to his
playmates, liking to know and do what they knew not and could not. He
sat still while his aunt threw handfuls of leaves into the firepit making
a smoke that filled the darkness of the hut. She began to sing. Her
voice changed sometimes to low or high as if another voice sang through
her, and the singing went on and on until the boy did not know if he
waked or slept, and all the while the witch's old black dog that never
barked sat by him with eyes red from the smoke. Then the witch spoke
to Duny in a tongue he did not understand, making him say with her
certain rhymes and words, until the charm came on him and ~~wouldd utte~~ held him still.
~~oolddae~~

"Speak!" she said to test the spell.

The boy could not speak, but he laughed.

Then his aunt was a little afraid of his strength, but she said
nothing. She threw clear water on the fire till the smoke cleared away,
and gave the boy water to drink, and when the air was clear and he ~~kid~~ could
~~could have voice~~ Speak again she taught him the true and secret name of the falcon, to which the
falcon must come.

This was Duny's first step on the way he was to follow all his life.

When he found that the wild falcons stooped down to him from the
wind when he summoned them by name, alighting with a beating of wide wings
on his wrist like the trained hunting-birds of a prince, then he hungered
to know more such names, and came to his aunt begging to learn the name
of the sparrowhawk and the osprey and the eagle. To earn the words of
power he did all the witch asked of him and learned of her all she taught,
though not all of it was pleasant to do or know. There is a saying on
Gont, ~~Weak as woman's magic,~~ Weak as woman's magic, and there is ~~another saying,~~ another saying, ~~Wicked~~ Wicked as woman's magic.
~~Now the witch of Ten Alders~~ Now the witch of Ten Alders was no black sorceress, nor

Q: Do you think of some animals — cats, for instance — as teachers or guides?

A: Absolutely. Guides to life, to death. The trouble with most of what you learn from animals is that it has, like the animals, no words — which is frustrating for wordy people such as writers. But then, that is exactly one of the things you learn from animals, that there is wordless knowledge.

Q: The wizards of Earthsea know the true names of things and that's what writers try to do too. Are there ways in which writers of fantasy can get at the true names more readily than can writers of "realistic" stories?

A: Well, it's far more direct for the fantasist. A Chekhov has to go through all that "thick description" of the real world, which the clarity of the true name scarcely can pierce through, in gleams and glimpses only (but all the more precious for that), and cannot be directly spoken. The fantasist can fly straight to the light. But had better, like a moth, watch out — circle round and fly back into darkness. Too direct, it's all lost. A puff of smoke. As a sort of do-it-yourself Taoist, I have to add that the name that can be spoken isn't the true name.

Q: Would you say why you think of the writer as a kind of discoverer and explorer?

A: The word *invent* (or even *making up*) has always seemed a little too intentional and deliberate for what I do, which feels more like finding things, coming upon them — places, people, patterns. But then, invention really does mean finding, coming to something, doesn't it? *Exploration* is a very good word for what one does when thinking about a story before writing and while writing it. You are exploring a territory, finding out what happens there. Only you do it with thoughts, images, words, instead of with your body.

Q: **What is a typical workday like for you?**

A: Sit at desk with computer, in rainy season. In fine weather, sit on deck with notebook. Three square meals.

Q: **Did you know as you wrote *A Wizard of Earthsea* that other, related books would follow?**

A: Not a clue. Only after a year or so did I look at the book and realize I had left all kinds of leads and hints for what might follow. That was a happy day. What next? Where is my wizard going now? What have they all been up to? What does this mean? Why is that as it is? It has been that way through all six books.

Q: **What role does revision play in your work?**

A: Sometimes immense. Other times, when the piece has "written itself," as they sometimes do, revision is fine-tuning, tinkering, fiddling, getting things right, linking things and picking up echoes and variations-on-the-theme throughout the story, getting the commas where they are needed and not where they're not. When major revision, rewriting, is needed, it is hard work, but never as hard as first-draft composition—not half.

I love revising, actually. Composing, although intensely exciting and rewarding, is hard and scary and exhausts both mind and body. Revising is just gravy. I have to make myself stop.

Q: **What do you tell young people who say they want to write?**

A: Read. Write. Read. Write. Go on reading. Go on writing.

Q: **What is the best part of being a writer?**

A: Writing!

AN URSULA K. LE GUIN READER

The Earthsea books:

> *A Wizard of Earthsea,* illustrated by Ruth Robbins
> (Parnassus, 1968)
>
> *The Tombs of Atuan,* illustrated by Gail Garraty
> (Atheneum, 1971)
>
> *The Farthest Shore,* illustrated by Gail Garraty
> (Atheneum, 1972)
>
> *Tehanu: The Last Book of Earthsea* (Jean Karl/Atheneum,
> 1990)
>
> *Tales from Earthsea* (Harcourt, 2001)
>
> *The Other Wind* (Harcourt, 2001)

Gifts (Harcourt, 2004)

MADELEINE L'ENGLE

Born 1918, New York, New York

Died 2007, Litchfield, Connecticut

FOR MANY YEARS, one of Madeleine L'Engle's favorite places was a simple, book-lined room above the garage at Crosswicks, her rural Connecticut home. It was in the quiet and privacy of that cozy hideaway, which she grandly named "The Tower" for fun, that L'Engle wrote several of the books that the world has come to know her by, including *A Wrinkle in Time*. In the downstairs living room at Crosswicks is the piano, once her mother's, which she played whenever work at the typewriter keyboard was not going smoothly. A short hike from the house is the large flat rock where she and her family had their picnics and where, at night, L'Engle spent hours on end watching the "living fire" of the sky as it filled up with stars "leading out into the expanding universe."

When L'Engle wrote *A Wrinkle in Time*, historical fiction and realistic novels about family life were the fashion as literature for young people. As a result, when L'Engle's most famous book was originally published, in 1962, it struck more than a few of its first adult readers as uncomfortably strange. Twenty-six publishers rejected *A Wrinkle in Time* before the author, who had begun to speak of it as the "book nobody likes," finally found an editor willing to take a chance on it. Then, to the surprise of many, *A Wrinkle in Time* won the Newbery Medal. This unexpected outcome for a book that L'Engle says she "had to write" proved to be one of the milestone events on the way to reawakening readers worldwide to the power of fantasy.

In her Newbery Medal acceptance speech, L'Engle said that one of fantasy's great appeals for her is that it is written in "the only language in the world that cuts across all barriers of time, place, race, and culture." Then she spoke about her passion for stargazing, described her favorite stargazing rock, and, quoting British astronomer Sir Fred Hoyle, concluded, "A book, too, can be a star, 'explosive material, capable of stirring up fresh life endlessly.'"

Leonard S. Marcus: What kind of child were you?

Madeleine L'Engle: I was an only child. Slightly lame. Couldn't run well. I was shy and gawky and didn't have many friends, so my imagination was very important to me. I was told that the first word I said was *clock*.

Q: Later you became an actress. How did you find the courage for that?

A: I just loved it. I began acting in high school. Onstage, I wasn't Madeleine. I became someone else — Sir Toby Belch, for instance. I would love to have played the great dramatic roles, but I was always a comedian.

Q: Did acting help prepare you to become a writer?

A: Yes. Because as an actor you hear words and see what they do, how words affect an audience.

Q: Your characters are something like an acting company: so many of them return in story after story.

A: I like that idea. But I didn't plan it that way. It just seemed natural to bring certain characters back. You know: you meet somebody and you like that person. You want to meet them again.

Q: Several of your characters are stargazers. What do you think about when you look up at the stars?

A: Sometimes I think about time. That the star I am looking at is that star as it looked a hundred or four hundred years ago. That when I stand here, in this time, and look at that star, I am not just looking at space. I am looking at time—at another time. That fascinates me.

Q: What was it like to write *A Wrinkle in Time*?

A: The story was unlike anything I had written before. Writing it felt wonderful.

Q: Did you know from the start how the story would end?

A: No. I've never done that! It is more fun not to know. If you know exactly what's going to happen, it doesn't work. But if you start to write the story and listen to it, see where it wants to go . . . well, I think that's how God creates.

Q: Did you know then that there was going to be a Time quartet?

A: I had no idea.

Q: Did you try out the manuscript on your own children?

A: Never. My children were seven, ten, and twelve at the time. But I didn't think to read it to them because I didn't think of it as being for children. That was my feeling at any rate. When people started calling me a "children's book author," I was very surprised. Baffled.

Q: Why had you wanted to write a story about young characters?

A: Because young people are still curious. They're still thinking and willing to change.

Q: What is your earliest memory?

A: It's New York. I'm wearing a dark brown legging suit and being taken for a walk to Central Park, where my nanny Mrs. O. bought some of that forbidden chewy stuff—caramel toffee. She thought I didn't have enough nice things to eat, and she had no hesitation about breaking rules if she thought it was a good idea.

Q: That's something you may have learned from her.

A: I learned a lot from her. Her name was Mary O'Connell. When I first knew her and I was a baby, I called her "O." And then "Mrs. O.," and it stayed "Mrs. O." Her life was not easy but she had a wonderful sense of humor.

Her daughter Harriet would read to me. I had a little case of English children's books, which my grandfather would send me, and the 1911 edition of the *Encyclopaedia Britannica*. She'd get awfully tired of the book, and I'd say, "You skipped a page!" Because she would have, and would then have to go back and read the page she skipped. Once I learned to read, I read anything I could get my hands on.

Q: You grew up with music all around.

A: My mother's mother had a beautiful singing voice. My mother played the piano. I think she did a little performing when she was young, but she hated to perform. She had stage fright. A different kind of shyness, I think, from mine.

When I was very young, my father took me to see *Madame Butterfly*. I thought it was just marvelous—but I wasn't prepared for an unhappy ending. So I said, "Is that all, Father?" And he said, "Yes. Well, did you like it?" And I said, " Oh yes, Father, thank you." And we went home, and he thought it was such a success that he took me to the next opera, which was *Pagliacci*. And we sat in our seats, and I said, "Father, does it have an unhappy ending?" And he said, "Yes." And I started to cry right there before the curtain ever went up, so he had to take me out. So I didn't go back to the opera for quite a long time.

Q: When did you first keep a journal?

A: I began when I was eight. What I wrote then was very dull. "Today I went to school and I hated it!"

Q: At least you knew your own mind.

A: Later, I read other people's journals and began to model mine on theirs.

Q: Were you a good student?

A: I was a very poor student. I had found that I wasn't being taught much about life in school, so I didn't pay much attention. I was in high school when I finally met a teacher who offered me encouragement as a writer.

Q: Was there a moment when you realized you were no longer a child?

A: One day when I was twelve, I looked in on my mother and saw that she was looking very sad. My mother up until then had just

Madeleine
L'Engle, age
ten or eleven,
in Breton
costume, in
Brittany,
France

been my mother. And suddenly I saw her revealed as a person. It was scary because she was unhappy. I hadn't realized that grownups could be unhappy.

Q: A fantasy version of that experience happens to Meg, in *A Wrinkle in Time*.

A: Yes. Meg gets a glimpse of her mother that she's never had before, and it comes from an unlikely source: the Happy Medium. It's fantasy, and yet it's the real reality. Something has to be true to be real, but it doesn't have to be real to be true.

Q: Do you like to read your manuscripts out loud as you work on them?

A: If I can, I read them to my grownup granddaughter, Charlotte. That's very helpful. You can't ask too many people for their opinions or you get confused. You pick one or two and listen to them but nobody else. My husband was my best editor. He was a great cutter. He would say, "You don't need that word." I'd say, "You're right." Then he'd say, "You don't need that sentence." And I would say, "All right. You want to cut the whole thing. Just cut it. Cut it all!"

Q: *A Wrinkle in Time* was rejected by twenty-six publishers. What was it like to have your work turned down repeatedly?

A: It was awful! I cried. I yelled. I stamped. I begged. It makes you think, Am I really a failure? Is what I think is so wonderful not wonderful after all? One editor said, "I may be turning down an *Alice in Wonderland*, but I'm afraid of it."

Q: When you finally did find a publisher, was your book completely finished? Or did your editor ask you to make changes?

A: I dropped one fairly short chapter, because they said the book was too long. And then I added another, much longer chapter! But it worked.

Q: Do you like to revise your work?

    A: I don't like to, but I do it. I do and do and do and do and do. I'm as lazy as anyone else. When I finish a book, I say, "That's it. I've done it!" And then I realize I have to do a lot more work. I scrawl my first draft and then I revise and revise and revise. I write in notebooks and type later.

Q: Your books have such vivid titles. Do they come easily to you?

    A: Titles are iffy. Sometimes I'm wonderful at it. Sometimes I'm terrible.

    My mother came up with the title *A Wrinkle in Time*. I went to take her her early morning coffee one day and she said, "I think I have a title for you right out of your text." And I said, "Oh, Mother, you've got it."

Q: How did you come up with the name for the planet Camazotz?

    A: Camazotz is a nasty South American god. I have a little book of names of gods of all religions. It's very useful.

Q: Has religion always been important to you?

    A: *My* religion has. World religion has not. I have always believed that if God made everything, he had to have liked it. I didn't want a God who hated me, who thought that babies were born in sin. I like some saints because they're funny. St. Theresa of Ávila, for instance, who was out in her carriage and got stuck in the mud. God said, "This is how I treat my friends, Theresa." To which she replied, "No wonder you have so few." I think we don't all have to think of God the same way.

Q: What is your workday like?

    A: I get up and I write—sometimes a short time, sometimes all day.

I never like not to be writing. It is living, eating, and breathing for me. I write with music playing—whatever happens to be on on the classical music station WQXR.

What happens is you've got to let your conscious and subconscious mind marry each other. My ideas come in the morning before I get up and at night before I slide into sleep. An idea for a story may sit around in me for years before I actually use it.

Q: What else, besides writing, do you enjoy?

A: I love to swim. Swimming has a definite rhythm, and writing should have, too. If you are using the rhythm in one aspect of your life, it makes it easier to feel it in other aspects of your life. If I hadn't swum, I probably wouldn't have written some of the things I've written.

Q: Do you sometimes get stuck while writing?

A: Every other page, probably.

Q: What do you do to get unstuck?

A: Play the piano. If I can't swim, I play the piano. If I can't play the piano, I listen to music. It breaks the barrier I've built up.

Q: What about research? Is that sometimes part of your work?

A: I enjoy research, although library research isn't that appealing to me because I like to write in the margins of the books I read, and you can't write in library books. I'll write, "No, I don't agree with you there!" Or, "Wow, that's just right. I think you're wonderful!"

I've been lucky and have traveled a lot. My husband and I once crossed the Mojave Desert, which was beautiful and far greener than I had expected. Later, I was able to draw on that experience when I wrote *Many Waters*.

Q: Why, in *Many Waters*, did you want to retell the story of Noah and the Flood?

A: I was living in the world at a time when we were very precarious. The idea that something could happen that would wipe out nearly everybody was perfectly possible and very frightening. In *A Swiftly Tilting Planet*, I had already written about the possibility of nuclear war. The two books are complementary in that sense. I'm dealing with the same thing in two different ways.

Q: Tell me about the impact of war on your life.

A: I have always been under the shadow of war. I've always been aware of it and afraid of it. I was born just after World War I. My father died because of that war. He had been gassed in the trenches and lived for seventeen more years, slowly coughing his lungs out. So I knew war was terrible. I would say to my father, "We're never going to have another war, are we, Father?" Well, he wouldn't lie to me.

To me the great villain was war. When World War II began, I was in my late teens. It was terribly conflicting. I didn't want to think that we should be involved, and yet I knew I couldn't sit back and let my Jewish friends be killed. So, we had to be involved.

Q: Do your feelings about war have something to do with why you have so often written fantasy?

A: Oh, yes. Fantasy was to me the way to write about it. There's the story of the princess who, whenever she was good and opened her mouth, beautiful things would come out. And whenever she was bad, nasty things came out: toads and snails. That's a story. The images may seem strange, but they make the meaning clear.

Q: Why do you write so often about unicorns?

A: I believe in unicorns. I always have. Unicorns keep coming into my work. I didn't study them. I learned about them inadvertently. There are a lot of ugly beasts. And I needed something to put up against the ugly beasts that was good, and that's the unicorn.

Q: Why do you write about multiple characters — the Murry twins, the Camazotz world of look-alikes in *A Wrinkle in Time,* the three Mr. Jenkinses in *A Wind in the Door*?

A: My mother had twin brothers. My father had twin sisters, and was a twin. So I'm surrounded by twins. And I expected to have twins, but I didn't.

Camazotz is the world they would like to push us into, where we all have to think the same thoughts, like the same music, eat the same foods. When a child or a grownup comes along who insists on doing it differently, that person is going to have a hard time.

Q: You were like that yourself as a child, weren't you?

A: Yes, without realizing it.

Q: And so is your character, Meg.

A: Of course. *I'm* Meg. I made her good at math, and I was good at English, but other than that . . .

Q: What do you tell children who say they want to write?

A: I say, "Write. That's the only way you'll find out. Just do it."

Q: Do you hear from many children about your books?

A: One eleven-year-old boy said to me once, "I read *A Wrinkle in Time.* I didn't understand it, but I knew what it was about." I loved that.

I had what started out as a very typical letter from a little boy, which ended, "P.S. I read your book (*A Wrinkle in Time*) while I was in bed. I have cancer." We corresponded until he died. It was hard and wonderful both. My books are not bad books to die with. What I mean by that is that when I read a book, if it makes me feel more alive, then it's a good book to die with. That's why certain books last.

Q: Are you a *Star Wars* fan?

A: Oh yes!

Q: Have you taken your grandchildren to see those movies?

A: I go alone or with a friend. I like to be free to scream, and I can't do that if I'm with the kids.

Q: Is fantasy writing more accepted now than it was when you were starting out as a writer?

A: Heavens, yes. I think that's because it's a scarier world. Fantasy gives you options. It's an attempt to touch on reality, in a way that can't be done better otherwise.

Q: What is the best part about being a writer?

A: Writing helps you to keep open and not close down. It helps you to keep on growing.

A MADELEINE L'ENGLE READER

An Acceptable Time (Farrar, Straus and Giroux, 1989)

The Time quartet:

    A Wrinkle in Time (Farrar, Straus and Giroux, 1962)

    A Wind in the Door (Farrar, Straus and Giroux, 1973)

    A Swiftly Tilting Planet (Farrar, Straus and Giroux, 1978)

    Many Waters (Farrar, Straus and Giroux, 1986)

The Young Unicorns (Farrar, Straus and Giroux, 1968)

GARTH NIX

Born 1963, Melbourne, Australia

M Y MOTHER," Garth Nix reports, "was reading *The Lord of the Rings* when she was pregnant with me. . . . Later my parents read it to me. I read it myself for the first time when I was seven and [among other times] at thirty-seven. I always find something new."

Nix belongs to the generation who grew up captivated not only by J. R. R. Tolkien but also by the mighty wave of *Rings*-inspired writers who were among Tolkien's earliest fans: Susan Cooper, Lloyd Alexander, Diana Wynne Jones, and others. He was five years old when *A Wizard of Earthsea* was a new book, and just one when *A Wrinkle in Time* won the Newbery Medal. In those days, Australia imported most of its literature and other culture from England and the United States. By the 1970s, however, when Nix was a teen-ager, Australia was coming of age as a place the world looked to for exciting new books, films, and architecture. Then as never before, an Australian teen could imagine making his mark as a writer.

Nix wrote portions of *Sabriel* while on a yearlong journey to visit a Syrian castle left over from the Crusades, Turkey's Roman ruins, and the fabled public gardens of Esfahan, Iran, among other places of special interest to him. In 1999, he became a full-time writer after having earned his living at a variety of jobs in government service, publishing, and marketing—"real-world" work that suited a writer who has always tried to "introduce a high level of reality" into his books. The best fantasy, Nix believes, lets us escape to "someplace else" while at the same time putting us in closer touch with "all sorts of human experiences . . . life, death, love, and tragedy. It's the best of both worlds."

Leonard S. Marcus: What kind of child were you?

Garth Nix: It's very difficult to look back at my younger self and describe him. I was a mixture of things, neither fish nor fowl. For example, I wore glasses from the age of eight or nine, was an avid reader, and a smart-ass, so I should have been a target for being bullied or picked on. But I was also quite large and strong and had a very bad temper (usually slow to come to the full boil). So I was never bullied at school, though perhaps this was also due to my good fortune in having very popular friends. I was neither popular nor unpopular myself, but a couple of my long-term best friends were the focal points of large social groups.

I wasn't very good at sports, though I played it as required. Team sports never interested me. I started fishing very young with my father, and it is still the only sport I really love and practice. I also cycled everywhere and did some long bicycle trips, but I wasn't interested in racing. Looking back, I think one of my defining characteristics as both man and boy is that if I can't be really good at something, I don't want to do it.

Apart from that, I was always a reader and always had a lively imagination. But I also knew when not to daydream and was good at practical and organizational things. I was a know-it-all in my preteens, a bit bossy in my early teens, and alternated between irritable and glum in my later teens. Apparently I always appeared self-confident even though I wasn't, particularly socially—though I was fine with most kinds of intellectual or practical challenges.

In short, I really don't know what kind of a child I was. Perhaps that is something that my family and friends could answer better, though I'm not sure I want to know.

Q: Were there storytellers in your family?

A: Both my parents used to tell us stories when we were children, my father in particular. He is a renowned leg-puller who has the advantage of being an eminent scientist. His tall tales tend to be based on fact or skirt the borders of reality, which means it can be very difficult to detect when he is making things up, even for members of the family.

Q: Did you enjoy school?

A: I enjoyed primary school. It was fun and not too onerous. I didn't mind the first few years of high school, but by fifth form (U.S.

grade 11, I think) I felt restricted by school. I just wanted to finish and get out into the world and be my own master (or so I imagined). I spent the first two months after school finished training with the Army Reserve and then went straight into a government job for eleven months, so I was quickly disabused of the notion of freedom! Mind you, after that I went traveling in the UK and Europe for six months, where I woke up each morning and decided where I wanted to go, or stay, and what I wanted to do.

Q: Was there a library that you, like Lirael, were eager to explore?

A: There was one particular library that was of great importance to me. It was very small, a single-story building rather like a garage, perhaps forty feet long and twenty feet wide. It was a dedicated children's library, on my walk between home and primary school. I stopped in every afternoon from the age of five or six to ten or so. It was an Aladdin's cave, a treasure trove of books. While it physically occupied just one big room, it was much bigger than that. The books in it changed every few months, and special orders could be made to the greater resources of the city's library service.

I remember the look and shape and texture of the editions I borrowed from that library and, on a recent visit to Canberra, was delighted to find some of those same editions for sale in a second-hand bookshop. They had those lovely library cellophane wrappers over the dust jackets, had (cancelled) Canberra Public Library Service stamps and cards in them, and from their general wear and tear could have been the identical books that I held in my smaller hands twenty-five-odd years ago. Needless to say, I bought them.

My school libraries were also important. I was delighted to dis-

cover at age seven or eight that it was possible to choose to go to the library for half an hour once a week instead of having a very Church of England scripture class. So, in company with several other early-developer agnostics, I went to the library and enjoyed uninterrupted book choosing and reading.

As an adult, I have become rather infected with the "if I like a book I must own it" syndrome, and so visit libraries less than book-stores, particularly secondhand bookstores. But I still love popping into a library and just wandering through the stacks.

Q: What were some of your first favorite books?

A: The earliest picture books I can remember that I loved were John Burningham's *Cannonball Simp* and *Trubloff*. I have vague recollections of a book with pirates but don't know what it was, and I think I loved *Where the Wild Things Are*, but perhaps I encountered it later.

The earliest novels I can remember really loving were *The Hobbit;* Arthur Ransome's *Swallows and Amazons* books; *Five Children and It, The Story of the Amulet,* and *The Phoenix and the Carpet* by E. Nesbit; and all the Moomintroll books by Tove Jansson.

Then there was the "golden age" of reading discovery between about nine and fifteen, when I re-read *The Lord of the Rings* and read as many books as I could get hold of by authors like (in no particular order) Robert Heinlein, Ursula Le Guin, Andre Norton, Rosemary Sutcliff, Ronald Welch, Alan Garner, Mary Stewart, John Christopher, Alexander Dumas, Patricia McKillip, C. S. Forester, Susan Cooper, Lloyd Alexander, Isaac Asimov, Diana Wynne Jones, Joan Aiken, Victoria Walker, and many more . . .

Q: When did you begin writing? When did you know that you wanted to be a writer?

A: My younger brother recently embarrassed me at a family Christmas dinner by producing a small booklet of stories that I apparently wrote and illustrated when I was about six or seven years old; my brother had found it while helping clean up a storage room at my parents' house. I didn't remember it at all, but my parents said I made a number of other books, including a kind of travelogue about a dragon's journey through Europe.

A part of my apprenticeship as a writer began when I was thirteen and started running games of Dungeons & Dragons for my friends. I was mostly the games-master, so I wrote the scenarios that were essentially blueprints for the adventures. It was very good training in narrative structure, particularly as the players could and would depart in new directions I had never thought of, and I had to make a story from what was happening in the game, not what I had hoped would occur or had planned for.

I wrote some articles and scenarios for role-playing game magazines in my late teens; they were my first paying market. But it wasn't until I was nineteen years old (in 1983) that I decided I wanted to try and write a book. I'm not sure I thought about the possibility of a career as an author; I doubt I thought beyond writing a book. I was traveling around the UK at the time in a beat-up Austin 1600, with a trunkful of favorite books and a Silver Reed portable typewriter. I started writing a fantasy novel and also wrote some short stories. One of the stories, called "Sam, Cars, and the Cuckoo," got me a telegram from Penguin Books in London; they wanted it for a magazine they published called *Warlock*, which was a marketing adjunct of their fighting fantasy game books. I was a bit puzzled at first, as I hadn't even sent them the story (the editor I had sent it to moved and took the story with him) but was very excited at the promise of publication and payment of the then extremely princely sum of about a hundred and fifty dollars. At the time I thought that if I wrote and sold a story every week or so I would be extremely comfortable. Sadly, while I wrote many short stories over the next eight years or so, I didn't sell any of them.

Garth Nix (right) at about age four, with his brother Simon

Q: How has growing up in Australia affected you as a writer? As a child, did you think of England as the "Old Kingdom," as a magical place?

A: Certainly the influence of English literature and tradition was very strong in my childhood, much stronger than it is for the current generation. Australian literature had its first mass flowering in the 1970s, when I was already a teenager. Before then, there were relatively few Australian authors and not much local publishing, and almost no Australian literature was taught in schools. England was to a large extent where books came from, and most of my favorite books were by English authors. My fascination with history also led me in the direction of England and Europe, and to a lesser extent the Americas and Asia. I never thought of England as a particularly magical place, but the depth of history there (and in Europe in general) was of great fascination to me, and still is, which is a kind of magic. This is hardly surprising since mainstream Australia, while geographically remote, is deeply connected to Western culture.

Aboriginal culture has an odd place in my psyche, as it does for many non-Aboriginal Australians. Certainly growing up, all the history we learned was of colonization as a good and useful activity, and what we learned of Aboriginal culture was very shallow and presented essentially as "quaint beliefs of savages." Later, as it became generally recognized that European settlement had in fact been a conquest and that the indigenous population was owed a debt, Aboriginal culture and its use or appropriation became a contentious issue. It isn't really possible now for a non-Aboriginal Australian to use or draw upon Aboriginal culture; this would be seen as yet another theft, this time of intellectual rather than actual property. So as an author, all that rich vein is off limits to me.

Q: Do you remember learning to tell time, or thinking about time as a child?

A: As I've said, history always fascinated me and as history is the "daughter of time," I guess I've always been fascinated with time as well. I don't remember learning to tell time as a child, nor do I have a great interest in time as a commonplace in our lives, or in its mathematical aspects. I don't care about "wasting" time or "managing" time. Time only interests me as a medium which encompasses what has happened, what is happening, and what will (or could possibly) happen.

Q: A common wish in fairy tales is to live forever. But your stories favor letting nature run its course. Is your interest in writing about death rooted in a deeper interest in nature?

A: I used to spend a lot of time in the bush, particularly in the years when I served as a part-time soldier in the Australian Army Reserve, and in addition to being out on exercises and so on, I did a lot of recreational bushwalking and cross-country skiing. I don't get much time in the bush now, but I still relish the rare opportunity to be away from people and under an open sky with just nature for company (and a few companions; I'm not a crazy hermit). I find that I cope with living in a city better if I can occasionally experience at least the illusion of wilderness, in a park or by the sea, till the next jogger comes past or a plane flies overhead.

I love sailing but haven't done much of it, apart from a course about six years ago when I first learned to sail. It's like many activities that I appreciate and enjoy and in theory plan to do more, but in reality I spend most of my time either writing or doing writing-associated things like interviews, publicity, and so forth, and just being a husband and father. At the moment I get out on a boat about once a year, I go fishing about three or four times a year, and I might do a short one-day hike in the bush even less often. While I've spent many nights under canvas or under the stars years ago, it's been quite a while since I've been on a hiking or cross-country skiing expedition. Nowadays my expeditions tend to be in my head more than actually out in the wilderness.

I do think that death is a natural part of life and that we should accept that. Obviously it is tragic and very sad when it comes unexpectedly or in traumatic circumstances, and such deaths can be very difficult for the living to cope with. But I don't think staving off death at all costs no matter the suffering involved is sensible or necessary. This doesn't mean I advocate letting nature take its course if you're sick or injured. I'm a firm believer in modern medical science, but if for example you've led a long and fruitful life and you're being kept alive in pain and suffering, then you should have the right to choose to die.

Q: Do you have a daily work routine?

A: I don't have a strict routine. I now have a separate office about ten minutes' walk from my home. I usually head off to that office somewhere between 8:30 A.M. and 10 A.M. I can choose to either walk along the coast through a small bay or along a street, as we live near one beach and my office is near another, with a small cove in between the two. That's a very pleasant way to start the morning. At the office, I often spend the morning doing administrative tasks; answering correspondence from publishers, publicists, and so on; doing e-mail interviews or the many other things that crop up,

Prepare illusion
Whiskers from rats
Tails made of cord
noses of cardboard an glued
~~threefinge~~ four-fingered gloves

↳ Takes most of the day

~~Approaching~~ O.W   Clanging on
                                       the hill

~~####~~ Wedged with some flotsam
in a gap.

"It can be done," said Scamandros. "But ~~I have nellows~~ shall have to begin from scratch, so it will take time. The first ~~th~~ing we will need are noses and tails."

"Noses and tails?"

"Yes, Rat noses and tails."

"Uh, I don't think —" Arthur ~~started~~ ~~say~~, ~~with a~~ look^ed at Longtayle and ~~the~~ Helmsvat, hoping they hadn't heard.

"No, no. Not real noses and tails. ~~We~~'ll have to make some, imbuing them ~~w~~ith sorcerous intent as we go. Now let ~~m~~e see. We'll need nice thin paper, ~~from~~ a simple glue, some cardboard, ~~a~~ctivated Ink."

As he spoke the Doctor pulled all these things out of his coat pockets, along ~~w~~ith a pair of scissors, several quill ~~pe~~ns, _____.

"Are you familiar with the common craft ~~k~~nown to many as papier-mache?"

"~~Er~~ Yes," said Arthur. He'd made masks

including running what is essentially a small to medium business. Sometimes I go home for lunch, or my wife and son come down to the office and we all have lunch at the beach. I then typically try to write in the afternoons, up to about 5:30 or 6:00 P.M. when I go home. Depending on where I'm up to with a book, I may then do some more writing at home between 9:30 P.M. or so and midnight. I used to write a lot more at night, but now our young son wakes me up too early, so I don't do much late-night writing at the moment.

Q: Do you know from the start how a book will end?

A: I usually have a general idea of how a story will end. Most often it is little more than a feeling or an emotion or an image, like a single still photograph, and the details turn up along the way. Sometimes I have a more detailed conception of where I want everything to end up, but even then it will be a grab bag of not-quite-worked-out ideas and story lines. I'm often quite surprised by how books come together at the end, particularly when I haven't consciously planned how all the plot lines will intersect and contribute to the ending.

Q: Do you revise your work?

A: Yes! I originally wrote longhand first, a chapter at a time, and then revised it as I typed it into the computer. Then I printed it out and went through it again, usually a couple of times at least. I still write difficult sections of my books longhand, but not all of the book. These days I typically write straight on to the computer, but then go through two, three, or four printouts, making corrections on paper, and then taking these corrections into the Word document. This is before the manuscript goes to the publisher, as of course there are more rounds of editing once the manuscript enters the publishing process.

One of my techniques with passages that don't seem to work is to read them aloud. This invariably shows up the weaknesses and infelicities in the prose. Words like *infelicities,* for example, show up as being redundant in my prior sentence.

Q: What was your "way in" to the writing of sequels to *Sabriel*? How did you realize you had more to tell?

A: There was mild pressure from my various publishers to write a sequel to *Sabriel* immediately. Not because it was a giant success at first, but it was critically well received. Then as it gathered momentum over time, the pressure increased. I ignored it initially, because the story in my head that I really wanted to write was what would become *Shade's Children.*

However, when I was partway through *Shade's,* I had an idea about a girl who lived with the Clayr in their glacier but who wasn't one of them. So I wrote some notes and a few short passages of description and dialogue. Over the next six months or so, I wrote some more notes, and a rough outline, and I became very interested in that story and started seriously working on it after I finished *Shade's Children.* Unfortunately for the waiting publishers and readers, after two or three years of writing, it ended up being too long and not quite right. With some editorial input and hair pulling and cursing at my end, I agreed that it should be split into two and that I needed to go back and tell more of Lirael's earlier story. So that big novel ended up in two volumes as *Lirael: Daughter of the Clayr* (the original title was just the subtitle), which was finished early in 2000 and came out in 2001, and then *Abhorsen,* which I finished very late in 2001 and was released in January 2003.

Q: Do you do research for your books?

A: I don't usually do much active research, in the sense that I don't make a list of topics or questions and then go and seek out the answers. But I'm always reading nonfiction books (particularly history and biography) and newspapers and magazines, and I soak up a great deal of information that quite often is a source of inspiration or ends up directly in my books. Occasionally I do check half-remembered facts to make sure I've got them right, or I look further into something I do know a little about, but feel I need more.

I also like browsing through reference books. My favorites are *Arthur Mee's Children's Encyclopaedia* (a constant source since I was about seven); *Brewer's Dictionary of Phrase and Fable* (a pre-1970 edition is best); *Encyclopaedia Britannica*; *A Dictionary of Chivalry* by Grant Uden, illustrated by Pauline Baynes; *The Oxford Companion to Ships and the Sea*; *The Nelson Dictionary of World History*; *The Century Cyclopaedia of Names*; and various old almanacs and other such reference works I have on the shelf closest to my desk.

Q: What do you tell young people who say they want to write?

A: Read a lot. Write a lot. Revise a lot. Submit a lot. Repeat all these steps. (Cribbed from Heinlein's advice to young writers.)

But also write what you love, not what you think is hot this year or has a better chance of selling. Write the stories and books that you want to read. If you want to write fantasy, then read history and nonfiction and other genres of fiction, not only fantasy, or you'll just be a copyist of the greats who have gone before. Read the great novels of the last two hundred years. If they've stuck around this long, there's always a reason.

Q: What is the best part of being a writer?

A: Making up stories. Finishing a book. Receiving the first copies, hot off the press. Having my work sit on the same shelves as books by authors whose work I have admired all my reading life.

A GARTH NIX READER

The Keys to the Kingdom series:
> *Mister Monday* (Scholastic, 2003)
> *Grim Tuesday* (Scholastic, 2003)
> *Drowned Wednesday* (Scholastic, 2005)

The Old Kingdom trilogy:
> *Sabriel* (HarperCollins, 1995)
> *Lirael: Daughter of the Clayr* (HarperCollins, 2001)
> *Abhorsen* (HarperCollins, 2003)
> *Across the Wall: A Tale of the Abhorsen and Other Stories*
>   (HarperCollins, 2005)

The Seventh Tower series:
> *The Fall* (Scholastic, 2000)
> *Castle,* illustrated by Steve Rawlings (Scholastic, 2000)
> *Aenir,* illustrated by Steve Rawlings (Scholastic, 2001)
> *Above the Veil* (Scholastic, 2001)
> *Into Battle* (Scholastic, 2001)
> *The Violet Keystone* (Scholastic, 2001)

Shade's Children (HarperCollins, 1997)

TAMORA PIERCE

Born 1954, Connellsville, Pennsylvania

G AZING OUT FROM her office window in the Manhattan high-rise apartment she shares with her husband and their cats, Tamora Pierce can see for miles. It's a commanding view, fit for one of her novels' triumphant warrior heroines. As a lookout from which to survey her adopted city, it also suits Pierce, who since childhood has had a passion for exploring the things that interest her from every conceivable angle.

As often as not, those interests—Japanese swordsmanship, the medieval code of knightly valor, the battles of the American Civil War—have in the past been considered primarily "guy" topics. Pierce is glad whenever one of her novels prompts a reader to question his or her ideas about what it really means to be a boy or a girl, a man or a woman.

Having grown up at the battlefront of her own parents' unhappy marriage, Pierce seems especially drawn to writing stories about young people who overcome difficult beginnings by finding strength and courage within themselves. Her heroines do so on a grand scale, in tales set in elaborately mapped and constructed imaginary realms where life often bears a striking resemblance to life during the Middle Ages. In Pierce's fantasies, wizards and shamans wield magical powers that lift the action above the everyday. Yet her stories satisfy in large part because they also are so down-to-earth. As Alanna tells her young shamans-in-training in *The Woman Who Rides Like a Man*, "The source of all your magic lies in your own will. Things happen because you want them to."

Leonard S. Marcus: What kind of child were you?

Tamora Pierce: I always had friends when I was very young, but by fourth or fifth grade I became more of a loner. We moved to the San Francisco Bay area from the East when I was in fourth grade. I had a hillbilly accent you could cut with a knife. Every time I opened my mouth, kids laughed at me. So I lost my accent, and that's when I started feeling outsider-ish.

"Walking Encyclopedia" was one of the many wonderful names the kids had for me. We were really poor, and one kid in sixth grade called me a "refugee from a rag bag." My parents' very ugly, long, bloody war for divorce went into full gear in my fifth-grade year and lasted through middle school. That was an additional stigma because in the 1960s people weren't getting divorced. My mother was a feminist. By middle school I was a feminist too, and that made me seem even weirder.

Q: Were you a good student?

A: My math, science, and gym teachers wouldn't have said so. The better math teachers were sort of resigned: they knew I was smart, and that I just couldn't do it. Science teachers—pretty much the same. Gym teachers—no! But English of course was my favorite subject. I liked social studies, languages, and art even though I was no good at it.

When I was ten I entered my "Egyptian Period"—read Egyptian mythology, and even handed in my school reports on scrolls! I majorly sucked at home ec. It wasn't supposed to be hard, but it was hard for me. I handed in both my apron and my dress—the big seventh- and eighth-grade home ec projects—eight weeks late, and they weren't very good. I did a lot better at learning how to write out checks! One of my cousins told me recently, "Oh, yeah. We'd all be on the floor playing doll babies, and you'd be off in a corner reading a book."

Q: What were some of your first favorite books?

A: When I was five or six, my mother put a package in my hands and said, "These are from your uncle Bob, and they're for you." I opened the package and there were four hardcover books about Winnie-the-Pooh—and they were mine! I still have chunks memorized. I *loved* them. The Dr. Seusses I had to share with my sisters. But these were mine, which was really important to me. I still chuckle inwardly at the silly stuff, like Pooh getting stuck in the honey jar.

Tamora Pierce,
age ten

My parents were both major readers, and they let me read whatever interested me. They did try to keep me from reading one book. It was about some English schoolgirls who thought they were very edgy and decided to set up a brothel! So I sat in the middle of the living room with the Sunday funnies up in front of my face—and the book inside.

Q: Were there good storytellers in your family?

A: Both my parents—and the whole extended family—told stories. We sang a lot at campfires and other get-togethers, and pretty soon somebody—usually it was my dad or Uncle Lyle—would start a story about our grandfather or the house where they'd grown up. One voice after another would pick up where the last person left off, and continue the story. It was just wonderful.

My dad's family—the Pierces and Prices—were from Appalachia. They were hillbillies, but I learned growing up that the television and movie stereotypes were dead wrong: these were smart people who were vastly inquisitive about things. As teenagers my dad and my uncle Lyle belonged to the Pennsylvania Historical Society. My granddad Sparks helped excavate the site of George Washington's first command—part of the retreat from the defeat at Bushy Run. So a love of history was a family tradition as well, and I came by my storytelling honestly.

Often my father would tell stories about wandering in the woods as a boy and finding historical artifacts. Or he'd tell stories about his experiences as a Ranger in the Korean War: a lot of funny ones, but as I got older, I also heard some of the harder stories. He didn't talk about the war easily. He'd also tell stories about Ike Swank, a river man who "once got trapped under ice three feet thick. But his teeth and jaws were so tough from years of chewing plug tobacco that he chewed his way out!"

Q: When did you start to write?

A: I always peg it at sixth grade because that's when my father heard me telling stories to myself at home one day, and suggested that I try writing a book. He recognized that I was a storyteller. That it meant so much to him was all I really needed for years and years.

But I was always pretty good at writing. When we moved to California, and I began to feel so out of place, I fell back on my imagination. I read and dreamed and wrote my own fiction. I won a newspaper contest with an essay on "What Christmas Means to Me" and had my picture in the paper and got twenty bucks. I had a really bad lisp that I finally beat in sixth grade. For my speech class, I wrote a fairy-tale story loaded with S's. I also wrote a lot of what is called "fan fiction"—I started with Tolkien and Robert Howard and Michael Moorcock. I told stories to my younger sisters at night. And when my mother worked for a local Head Start program and I was in high school, I also told stories to the kids there.

Q: Do you remember how you first found out about *The Lord of the Rings*?

A: My wonderful seventh-grade teacher Mary Jacobsen introduced me to Tolkien. She was also my safe haven during the years of my parents' divorce. She was one of those small, peppery women who suffers fools ill. When I noticed that about her, it made me appreciate all the more her giving me her time. One Friday afternoon I was looking at the books along the shelf in her room and engaging in my usual complaint—"I don't have anything to read!"—when she said, "Well, here. Try this," and handed me *The Fellowship of the Ring*. I went home and started reading. Saturday morning, around two A.M., I finished—crying, because I thought there wasn't any more. On Monday morning, Mrs. Jacobsen gave me the other two books. And that was when I started writing fantasy.

Q: What did you think of *The Lord of the Rings*?

> A: Tolkien was earthshaking. It was about great causes and about dying nobly, which interested me a lot for some reason. It left me all weak-kneed. I re-read the books at least once or twice a year until I was twenty-one or twenty-two. I was a major fan!
>
> So Tolkien is where I started. But in a way everything I write now is a contradiction to what I found in Tolkien. After a while, I noticed that in the real world there was no such thing as Good versus Evil. And I noticed that I didn't know any pale, noble, suffering, dignified people like Tolkien's characters—anybody ethereal. I didn't know anyone, like Gollum, who was all black and gnarly and fled in the light. Everybody I knew went to the bathroom! Nobody in Tolkien had a sense of humor, except Sam, who was a servant. I'm the kind of person who makes bad jokes in hospitals. And of course Tolkien was all about male heroics.

Q: Did other teachers encourage you?

> A: Each year there was always at least one who made it really clear that they thought I had something of worth to me. And in every school I ever went to, the school librarian and I were buds within the first month of my starting there.
>
> I got a lot of my enthusiasm about military history from my father. Then in college, after seeing my first martial arts movie, I read a great deal about Samurai Japan. What really put the hook in for me, though, was Ken Burns's television documentary *The Civil War*. Especially after hearing the quotes from William Tecumseh Sherman, the Union general, I got fascinated by the war and started

reading everything I could find about military history in general. It just went crazy after that! You get hold of one end of the string and you just keep following it. I ended up with all this stuff in my head that I used to think was not useful at all but now know, of course, that it is.

And that's why I tell schoolchildren: You know those things that you feel you have to know everything possible about—crocheting or dressage or ballet—and you go after it hammer and tongs for six or eight months and then get interested in something else and you go after *it*? And your parents say you have no follow-through? Actually, you're laying the base for your creativity. That obsession may not seem important now, but you'll be able to draw on it later.

Q: Did you just keep writing from fifth and sixth grade on?

A: When I was in tenth grade, all my teachers were pounding it in to me to "Write what you know, write what you know." They meant it in the narrowest possible way. I was bored by real life. But I tried to do it anyway—and then I sent my story to *Seventeen* magazine. The editor wrote back a wonderful letter saying that although she couldn't publish my story, she could see that I was very talented and that I should keep on writing. My mother asked me why I had gotten a letter from *Seventeen,* and when I told her, instead of being proud of me, as I had expected, she went off on me, saying, Who was I to think I was good enough to be published? Who did I think I was? I was *never* going to get published. I was a second-rater. And on and on. It was after that incident that I tried to run away. And I didn't write any more original fiction for another five years.

My mother was a brilliant woman who just gave up, and anything

I did that led her to think I might be trying to go beyond the limits she had set for herself was trouble. What I've learned is that there are always going to be plenty of people who are going to tell you that you suck. At a certain point you've got to believe them or—my husband and I use this "Weird Al" Yankovic song title as our motto—you've got to "Dare to Be Stupid." That's how you set yourself free. My mother never could do that.

Q: How did you get back to writing stories?

A: In college, I took a fiction writing class with a novelist named David Bradley, who suggested that I write a book about my childhood. But when I started going dry after five pages, I thought, Okay maybe what's important now is not *what* I write my first book about but *that* I write a first book—and make the leap. Then I thought about what it was that I used to write about, when I was younger and writing was as easy as breathing. The answer was: girl fantasy heroes. So I sat down and I started to write about a girl who disguises herself as a boy to win the tournament, to become the prime minister. It stank! It was *dig-a-seven-foot-hole-at-the-crossroads, wrap-it-in-lead-foil, bury-it-in-the-hole, cover-the-hole-with-asphalt-in-the-dark-of-the-moon, with-a-stake-driven-through-it* BAD! But, at 112 pages, I'd broken through the wall. It was a book. Five months later, I sat down with a fragment of an idea and started to write about another girl warrior disguising herself as a guy. Five months and 732 manuscript pages later, I had *Alanna*.

I stayed with it because I was writing what I wanted to read: girls kicking butt, mainly. That's a requirement. In my books, boys can kick butt too—and even adults if they behave themselves. But for years and years we've been so brainwashed into thinking that males and females have two different roles, and I think we're all going to be a lot happier in our lives if we start looking at the things we have in common. I try to show this through my books, and a story about a girl in a man's field is still one of the clearest contrasts you can present as a writer.

Q: Do you sometimes model your characters on people you know?

A: When I started out, I did because I knew what they looked like and how they talked. I'm not comfortable making stuff up. I'm not good at it. Alanna is based on my sister Kim, who is five years younger than me. Her first word was "No!"—and I knew she meant it because her teeth were buried in my finger at the time. One of my coolest memories is of Kim when she was first old enough to tell *me* stories.

Kim was the rebel against my mother. I got my intellectualism from my mother. Even after my mother gave up on making something of her life, she still had interests that ranged wildly over everything. In part because I was like her in this respect, I could never hate her the way my sisters did. Kim was the one with the courage to run away. I tried once, but came back right away. But Kim started trying to run away when she was twelve, and she made it out successfully by the time she was thirteen, when she went to live with my dad. Melanie left when she was fourteen. I was in college by then. Kim is multitalented, a real genius, and has a real fighting spirit. So she was perfect for Alanna.

I based the Lord Provost in *Lioness Rampant* on my dad. He kept telling me to write a part for a mean old biker, and I kept explaining,

rotted = tooth

sighting on Kel with a grin.

White light blazed around her: Prosper's work. The men at the ~~base~~ [foot] of the ~~cliff~~ [trail]
threw up their hands to shield their ~~lives~~ [eyes]. Kel ~~continued to~~ back [up] [Kel], sweating and trembling.
She ~~didn't even have the option of simply~~ [couldn't just] watching her feet, as she did on stairways. She
had to focus on the men at the ~~foot of the trail~~ [trail's end], which meant seeing how narrow the ~~trail~~ [path]
itself was, and how far she would fall before she hit the ground. That distance only got
larger as she carefully sidled upward.

Two raiders dismounted. She could see they were thinking of ~~taking her~~ [followins]: their
swords were out, their eyes ~~were~~ locked on her. She ~~made herself~~ [held] halt, and turn [ed to] ~~so she~~
~~completely blocked the trail.~~ [She stands steady, she lowered] Her spear was out in front of her, the point steadily toward the
men below ~~though her heart was in her throat at the thought of~~ [Her Yamani training covered her fear of] the drop just inches from her
right foot. Jump walked between her legs [spread] to stand before her, growling. ~~He was cut in a~~
~~few places and~~ his muzzle was crimson with blood, a sight guaranteed to make the ~~bravest of~~ [m]
men think twice.

Then Kel's sparrows ~~were there~~ [arrived], div[art]ing at the men at the foot of the path. The[y] [bandits]
yelled and backed off, trying to protect their ~~eyes~~ [faces].

"Jump, go _now_," Kel ordered. The dog ~~turned and~~ ran between her legs and on up
the trail. Kel pulled her right foot back from the drop, sweat running down her ~~forehead and~~
cheeks. She ~~couldn't even shake it from her eyes for fear of stepping wrong.~~ If I don't
move, they'll ~~fill~~ [shoot] me full of arrows ~~where I stand~~ [right here], and then I'll _really_ fall, she told herself,
and ~~moved~~. ~~Now she slid~~ [turned to sidle] up the trail, her back hugging [against] the rock face, her eyes on her feet.
Two more bursts of light ~~as she climbed~~ [I kept the bandits milling & half-blind] signaled that Prosper was ~~still looking out for her~~.

"Pa, they don't have Harleys in Tortall." He and my ma—my step-mother—had started the Idaho Motorcycle Club. They both drove Harleys. Pa kept saying, "I don't care. Write me a part." So there is a moment at the end of *Lioness Rampant* where the Provost says to Alanna, "You take care of your end of things?"—meaning, Did you do your job?—and she says, "Indeed I did," and they both grin "wolfishly." That moment in the story was for me, because that is the moment when Buri recognizes that the Provost and Alanna have a family resemblance. Ma became the Shang Wildcat who taught Kel and who met Alanna in *Lioness Rampant*. I pretty well drafted my whole family.

I have also based my characters on actors and performers because once again I know how they look and sound and move. Now I also go into world magazines and world photo books, clip photos, and post them in my office. I keep files and files of pictures of people. Every time I need a new character I go through the appropriate files broken down by age, sex, and ethnicity and "cast" my character. For *Tris's Book* in the Circle of Magic quartet, I needed a head of the Fire Temple, which is in charge of defense, and I modeled the character on General Sherman: the short red hair, the barking laugh.

Q: Do you have a daily work routine?

A: In the morning I usually work on correspondence and e-mail, or play with the cats. My assistant comes in two days a week. I like to have lunch with fans. Early afternoons I tinker and post on my Sheroes Central website [an Internet discussion site cofounded by Pierce and Meg Cabot]. I start writing around three, but it doesn't really start to click until around four.

First, I go over what I wrote the day before, partly to get myself in the mood and partly to do a first rough edit. I set myself a daily page quota: about five pages when my deadline is still far off; as much as twelve to fourteen pages when it's getting close. If I don't make my page quota, I can't watch TV. Usually by eight o'clock or so, when my favorite programs come on, I'm done.

Q: What do you do when you get stuck?

A: I'll get up and go read a bit. If I'm really having a hard time, I'll go run errands and set a time on the clock to put the butt back in the chair.

Q: Do you know from the start how a book will end?

A: I have a rough idea. The beginnings for me—the first four or five chapters—are like the opening scenes of a movie: they're going to introduce the theme of the book, and the main characters are going to meet. Writing my first chapter always takes at least three times as long as the next two. Endings are fairly basic for me. There's a forest fire. There's a flood. The ground opens up. The palace collapses. Pretty easy. But then there's the middle, where all my ducks from the beginning have to line up just right to get through to the palace collapsing. That's usually when I scream for my husband, Tim. Because he's lived in the universes of my books as much as I have, we can talk about the characters together. That really helps a lot.

Q: Do you do research for your books?

A: When I was six or seven, there was a TV show about Robin Hood that I loved. As soon as I learned how to read, I looked up "Robin Hood" in our *World Book Encyclopedia*. At the end of the entry it said, "See also the Crusades." So I read that entry too, and from the time

I was seven until the time I was ten or so, I read everything I could find—fiction or nonfiction, I didn't care—about the Middle Ages. So when I sat down and wrote the original manuscript that became the Song of the Lioness quartet, I didn't need to research. I just sat and I wrote.

Nowadays, I'll take any reference to a medieval craft or skill that comes up in the books as the excuse to find out more about it—how jousting was done, where exactly a knight on horseback rested the butt of his lance when he wasn't actually using it. To learn the answer to that question, I went to the Arms and Armor Department at the Metropolitan Museum of Art in New York. But when I looked at the display [of full suits of armor mounted on life-size models of horses], I saw that the lances were resting on bits of metal that obviously weren't authentic. I'm still mad at the Met for that! Fortunately, my editor was on vacation in France just then and was able to send me back posters of a medieval tapestry that answered my question. More recently, through Sheroes Central, I have gotten to know a woman who jousts at the New York Renaissance Faire, in Sterling Forest, New York. So now I can ask her some of my questions, like how long a horse can stand up to that kind of combat. It's cool to have a living source.

Q: Do you revise your work much?

A: When I'm close to finishing a book, I'll start printing out copy and go over it by hand. I see things on the paper manuscript that I didn't see on the screen. If I have time, I'll read it aloud as well. Then I hand it in. That's one draft for me, and then there is the usual back and forth with my editor.

Q: What do you tell young people who say they want to write?

A: I say that you have to find your own way of doing things. One reason that I read so many books about how other writers work is that I want to be able to tell kids, "So-and-So does it this way. So-and-So does it this other way. And I do it still another way." I want kids to realize that there are a variety of possibilities and that we all have to try different things to keep learning.

I say, Immature artists imitate; mature artists steal! And I say, If you don't like something you wrote six months ago, that's good because it means you have been getting better as a writer. I say that my own favorite book is the one I've just published because it is the one in which I feel I got the most things right.

I say, Write what you're most comfortable writing, whether it's fantasy stories or nature stories or something else. I also say, The hardest and most important thing to learn is to listen to your gut. That's really hard because your gut is really quiet and a lot of other things are really loud. But the thing that makes you want to write knows a lot more about what it's doing than you do, and you have to find some way to trust that thing, even when you're telling yourself, "I stink!" And I say, Keep writing. When I was starting out, I would have killed for five minutes with a working writer who could have helped me with even one of the things I was struggling with— like, How do you come up with names?

Q: How *do* you come up with names?

A: Names are tricky for me. I have twenty-two baby name books, plus three URLs for baby name databases, plus a CD-ROM, plus all the names I've collected over the years. It's not like I'm obsessed or anything! I look for names that feel right to me. I started out at a time when fantasy books had characters with names that were ten syllables long, with accent marks and apostrophes. I got to the point, in the 1970s, where if I saw a name like that on the back of the book, I didn't buy it. I wanted fantasy to be real. So I started out using real names. Unfortunately, early on it showed: Alex, Gary, Jonathan. Nowadays, I'll go for a name from a different culture, or with a name I've tweaked a little in some way.

Q: What is the best part of being a writer?

A: Knowing when I write something that I think is pretty cool that there are a bunch of people who are going to think it's pretty cool too. Being able to show kids, especially kids who come from poverty or from dysfunctional homes, that it is possible not only to survive but also to succeed. Turning a corner in a story and finding some incredibly cool character that I didn't know was going to be there. I think that's the best part.

A TAMORA PIERCE READER

The Circle of Magic quartet:
Sandry's Book (Scholastic, 1997)
Tris's Book (Scholastic, 1998)
Daja's Book (Scholastic, 1998)
Briar's Book (Scholastic, 1999)

The Circle Opens quartet:
Magic Steps (Scholastic, 2000)
Street Magic (Scholastic, 2001)
Cold Fire (Scholastic, 2002)
Shatterglass (Scholastic, 2003)

The Daughter of the Lioness books:
Trickster's Choice (Random House, 2003)
Trickster's Queen (Random House, 2004)

The Immortals quartet:
Wild Magic (Jean Karl/Atheneum, 1992)
Wolf-Speaker (Jean Karl/Atheneum, 1994)
The Emperor Mage (Jean Karl/Atheneum, 1995)
The Realms of the Gods (Jean Karl/Atheneum, 1996)

The Protector of the Small quartet:
First Test (Random House, 1999)
Page (Random House, 2000)
Squire (Random House, 2001)
Lady Knight (Random House, 2002)

The Song of the Lioness quartet:
Alanna: The First Adventure (Atheneum, 1983)
In the Hand of the Goddess (Atheneum, 1984)
The Woman Who Rides Like a Man (Atheneum, 1986)
Lioness Rampant (Atheneum, 1988)

TERRY PRATCHETT

Born 1946, Beaconsfield, England

O NCE YOU LEARN about magic," says Miss Tick, the witch who becomes young Tiffany's mentor in *The Wee Free Men,* "I mean really *learn* about magic . . . then you've got the most important lesson still to learn. . . . Not to use it." Magic, as Miss Tick explains, is not only hard work. It can easily spin out of control. On most occasions, it is better simply to use your head, to pay close attention to "everything that's going on," and—for good measure—to take delight in life's little details. As a recipe for living, Miss Tick's advice makes as much sense for nonmagical folk as it supposedly does for witches. It also comes close to capturing the particular flavor of Terry Pratchett's own way of seeing the world.

Pratchett published his first story as a thirteen-year-old and his first book of fantasy, *The Carpet People,* ten years later. In 1983, he wrote the first of an ongoing series of loosely related satirical fantasies about Discworld—a wildly chaotic, free-floating realm populated by outlandish villains, fools, and occasional heroes, all of whom are easy enough for us to recognize. Tiffany, for instance, although far from the kindest, most well-mannered girl you might hope to meet, proves her worth not only by saving her brother but also—just as important in Discworld terms—by opening her eyes to the truly amazing strangeness and muchness of life: "I worked it out," as she tells Miss Tick and her witch companions at last. "*This* is . . . the magic place. The world. Here. And you don't realize it until you look."

Leonard S. Marcus: What kind of child were you?

Terry Pratchett: I was an only child and probably a very typical one. I had my own room, and I didn't have to share—not that there was that much to share. Because there was a whole bunch of kids of about the same age who went around the village in various gangs and groups, I also had enough company. I felt kind of like an only child with lots of brothers and sisters. So, in a sense, I had the best of both worlds.

I was born on the Chiltern Hills, which are chalk, and I remember when it dawned on me as a kid that the chalk we were digging up was really *dead things*—the shells of dead creatures. It didn't horrify me. It struck me as kind of wonderful. The chalk had formed on the bed of an ancient, deep sea, and I used to walk around thinking that I could kind of *feel* that sea underneath me. I could make myself quite dizzy with the thought of deep time—that what I was walking over was a physical analog of time. Of course I wouldn't have been able to say it that way then.

Q: Did growing up in the years after World War II affect your life as a child?

A: I was born because of the war. My uncle, who was then a small boy, was evacuated from the East End of London down to the country. His big sister used to come and visit him at the house where he was staying. And she met a handsome young man, the son of the gardener, who was in the Royal Air Force. He was my father. She was my mother. They married, and then he went off to India. So the war changed a lot of lives, ended many, and started some.

After the war, my father worked as a motor mechanic. My mother used to do the books for local firms. We were poor but we didn't know it, because most people were. If you had a house that hadn't been bombed, you were ahead of the game.

We lived down in the country and were the last generation to grow up before television was a major force. We were a gang of kids running around, having fun, getting dirty—and always safe. We had trees and orchards. The only thing we didn't have was a pond where you could put a raft—and possibly drown!

Q: Did you enjoy reading?

A: I didn't read children's books until I was ten. In fact I read as few books as I could possibly get away with. Then my uncle gave me a copy of *The Wind in the Willows,* and I read it at one sitting. I didn't know there *were* books like that. It is a seriously weird book, and as a kid something about that communicated itself to me. I went from being a kid who didn't read to—just a week or so later—being a kid who wanted to read absolutely everything there was in the whole world. It happens like that.

Q: Did you read Mary Norton's *The Borrowers*?

A: Yes, but I didn't like the Borrowers much. They seemed to be a bit too bourgeois, and I didn't have the sense of where this little family had come from. There were these few families. They didn't seem to have any communication with others. It all seemed artificial.

People about six inches high are fairly commonplace in English children's books. I remember reading a marvelous book called *Mistress Masham's Repose* by T. H. White, which I recall with extreme fondness because the Lilliputians were treated as real—as living and breathing, as having an economy. They thought in terms of a kind of civilization. There's a lot of *Truckers* in them: the feeling that these are not toy people. They're just the same as us, but small. I also read John Masefield's *The Box of Delights* and *The Midnight Folk*, and E. Nesbit and Tove Jansson.

Q: Did you, like Tiffany in *The Wee Free Men,* think of fairy tales as unreal?

A: As a kid I kept coming up with things like, It must have been a really big oven to put a whole boy in. It struck me as odd that there was only one foot in the whole of the kingdom for the glass slipper. You know: size 7¼. How hard can that be? I applied logical laws where logic shouldn't be applied. I saw things in the stories that I wasn't supposed to see and that it was fun to find. A lot of the humor of Discworld has derived from taking the logical view.

Q: Tiffany reads a dictionary all the way through. Did you do that as a child?

A: The first book I ever asked my parents for was a dictionary. The first book I remember buying for myself, when I was eleven, was E. Cobham Brewer's *Dictionary of Phrase and Fable*.

Some of Tiffany was straight from the heart because, like her, I was a kid who very quickly had a reading vocabulary much, much bigger than my spoken one. So, I actually did believe that there was a kind of ghost called a pa-han-tom [phantom] and a kind of monster called an oh-gree [ogre].

Q: Did you enjoy school?

A: They taught me to read. They taught me the multiplication tables up through 12 times 12. And I suppose they taught me to write. But I don't recall any of my school days with much pleasure. I was just high enough up the ladder not to be noticeable. And I always had the feeling that I'd done something wrong. No one was going to tell me what it was—and I was going to get punished for it. I hated the place! When I was still in the school for younger kids, my mother, God bless her, told me about the water cycle: how rain is formed and evaporates off the surface of the sea and becomes clouds, and how the clouds then blow over the land and cool down, and it rains. I was very pleased to know this. Then one day in school, when I was about seven, the teacher asked us, "Who can tell me where rain comes from?" I thought, This is it. I know this one! And I raised my hand and said, "It comes from the sea." And she said, "Don't be silly. It comes from the sky." I hope there's a circle in hell for teachers like that. There was no attempt to ask, "Why is this kid saying this?" It was just, "You're wrong!" But I wasn't wrong, and I knew I wasn't.

Q: Was there a local library where you lived?

A: It was when I found the local library that my real schooling began.

They gave me four tickets, which meant that I could borrow four books at a time, and I thought this was ridiculous. So after a few weeks I went to see the head librarian and I said, "Can I come and work here on Saturdays?" He said, "Well, if you want to help out that's fine." I was quite good and did all the chores—and they turned a blind eye to the fact that I now had 146 library tickets. I would write them out myself. Children were not expected to be in the adult section of the library, but because I was an honorary librarian I was also an honorary adult. So I pillaged the science fiction shelves, such as they were. There weren't too many science fiction books, but I found them all. And then I started in on the fantasy books and the folklore, because they kind of looked like fantasy. Then I started in on the mythology, because that looked like fantasy too. And then ancient history, because, you know, it's the guys with helmets and swords—like fantasy again. And so I got educated by one thing leading to another. What was nice was when facts I came upon began to cross-reference with others I had already learned, when a web of knowledge started to form.

Q: When did you start to write?

A: I went to my first science fiction convention when I was thirteen. Giants like Arthur C. Clarke would come to these conventions. You could meet with them and chat with them—if you weren't completely weird!—and there was always this tacit encouragement to try your hand at writing. And that's how I started. I wrote my first short story that same year. My school magazine published it. The other kids liked it. Suddenly I had my ticket into the gang because I could make them laugh.

Q: Do you think now of fantasy as being useful in some way?

A: Fantasy is like an exercise bicycle for the mind. It might not actually take you anywhere, but it does exercise the muscles that will. I especially enjoy writing the stuff that questions the received opinion. So, when Tiffany reads that the witch in the fairy tale is "wicked," her response is to think, Where's the *evidence?*

Q: Was Granny Aching, about whom you write with such affection, based on a real person?

A: Bits of real people. Bits of my father's mother, with whom I used to spend the summer holidays. You pick up a lot of stories and odds and ends from your grandparents. It's the grandparents who have got the time to tell stories while the parents are out working. But

Granny Aching also grew out of observation—I couldn't tell you of what—and she arrived almost fully formed in my mind. So I would have to say that she was made up—but spun out of real things.

Q: *The Wee Free Men, The Amazing Maurice,* **and the Bromeliad Trilogy are all stories about knowledge being passed on from generation to generation.**

A: A fact I treasure knowing—in the same way that Tiffany treasures knowing the word *susurrus*—is the fact that my father was a boy when Wyatt Earp died. People usually think of Wyatt Earp as an "historical character"—not contemporary with anyone now alive. But the fact is that he died in 1929, when airplanes were no longer rare things—and my father was seven or eight. I think it's amazing to realize that there really are these links between what we would call "a long time ago" and the present. It gives you a handle on what time is. I like to measure time in "grandfathers"—the average difference in age between a young child and his grandfather, or about fifty years. It doesn't take many grandfathers to bring you back to Napoleon.

Reading about the American West is my hobby. To me, the old West is a fantasy world that has the added bonus of being real. As a fantasy writer, I find there is no better way of spending my time than reading social history or eyewitness history.

Q: **In** *Truckers,* **you describe another "real" fantasy world—a department store.**

A: That goes back to a specific memory from my childhood. Picture this scene. When I was six years old, we had no electricity in our house, just gas lamps and oil lamps. Six years old, I go on a train for the first time, a steam train to London. I go to a huge department store. It's Christmas time. In London, there is not just electricity but all the Christmas lights. There is a shop with more toys than I could have possibly imagined existed. We go to see Santa Claus. He is sitting in a kind of wooden airplane. You get in one side and get out by the door on the other side: an entire trip to the North Pole and back in about fifteen seconds. At one point my mother lost me, and when she found me, I was going up and down on the moving staircases, with my mouth open, just looking up. I was having instant sensory overload: all the noise and the color and the sparkling hitting me at once. *Truckers* was written by that kid, that small kid in a big store that was full of things he didn't understand but were absolutely amazing.

Q: Tiffany sounds like she's talking about "sensory overload" when she tells herself, "No wonder we dream our way through our lives. To be awake, and see it all as it really is . . . no one could stand that for long."

A: Some years back, four enormous pieces of ice slammed into the planet Jupiter. We saw that on television, and the BBC went out and interviewed people in the street. When they asked an old lady whether the news worried her, she said, "Oh, no. That's the kind of thing that happens in outer space." But once you realize that *we're* in outer space too, and that what happened before will happen again, then you begin to loosen up a bit from the mundane, everyday realities. The trick is to hold that realization in your mind while also taking care of business.

We all have those moments of absolute clarity. But if we had nothing but those moments, we'd just sit there all blissed out on the mere fact that the grass is green. We have to know how to keep the "Wow!" in its place.

Q: And making up stories is part of how people do that?

A: Yes, because making up stories enables you to feel a certain measure of control. It's a very human thing to do. I think it's what defines us.

Q: Did your work as a reporter help prepare you to be a writer of fantasy?

A: On my very first day, I saw my first dead body and learned that it's possible to go on throwing up even after you've run out of things to throw up. Being a reporter taught me not to be frightened of the blank page. I learned that a word that is not read is a word that hasn't been properly written. I learned to produce because if you don't produce, unsympathetic editors come and shout at you. I saw all kinds of people in all kinds of circumstances—often in circumstances where perhaps they'd prefer not to be seen—in the courtroom, for example. All of which is damn good training for a writer.

Q: Do you do research for your books?

A: While I was writing *The Amazing Maurice,* I read a book written by a Victorian rat catcher, and I looked up various facts about Rat Kings. Over the years, I've built up a huge reference library, and if I needed some interesting facts about chocolate in the nineteenth century, I could probably go find them in some book I already have. I also find that when a book is really beginning to work well, *everything* I encounter suddenly seems to have some relationship to it. It's almost as if my brain has been tuned. I will overhear a conversation or read a brief news item in the paper that directly affects what I'm writing. The stuff finds you. It's rather like Tiffany opening her eyes again.

Q: Tell me about the magic in your books.

A: If you use magic in fiction, the first thing you have to do is put barriers up. There must be limits to magic. If you can snap your fingers and make *anything* happen, where's the fun in that? In *A Hat Full of Sky*, which is the second book about Tiffany, I have her learning what might be called the "hard end" of witchcraft, which is being a combination of village midwife, wise woman, and nurse. It means that you are giving all the time, that other people are taking, and that you don't get much rest, and it isn't what you think witchcraft is going to be when you set out. There's an awful lot of dirt and bandaging and looking after people, and not very much broomstick. Discworld is a magical place, but very little actual magic happens. When Tiffany magically turns someone into a frog, it turns out to be a very horrifying moment because of the law of the conservation of mass. You get about two ounces of frog and all the matter that's left over takes the form of this kind of big pink balloon floating up against the ceiling, making "gloop, gloop" noises. It's all very messy. The story really starts when you put limits on magic. Where fantasy gets a bad name is when anything can happen because a wizard snaps his fingers. Magic has to come with a cost, probably a much bigger cost than when things are done by what is usually called "the hard way."

Q: Do you have a daily work routine?

A: I assume that what I'm doing is writing all the time—even though I'm actually doing something else. When you are stuck and you go out into the garden to pull weeds, you are still writing. Part of you is. That's why it's vitally important to have a notebook beside your bed. Often the resolution of a difficult bit that I wrote the day before, and that I was stuck on, will trot along in front of my eyes when I'm lying in bed just waking up. So writing isn't just sitting in front of the keyboard, although that's a fairly vital part of the process. You're still being a writer when you are reading or making notes, or just enjoying yourself.

Q: Do you revise your work?

A: My books go through five drafts. Draft Zero is something I would never show anyone! Draft One is me telling the story to myself once I think I know how it goes. Draft Two is me telling the story to my editor. Draft Three is what we end up with. And Draft Four is what I call sanding and polishing—when the spell checker comes into play and I'm working on the fine detail of sentences. The trouble is, at any given time, parts of the manuscript may be up to Draft Four and others still in Draft Zero. The whole thing looks like some kind of permanently changing patchwork. But it all works out eventually.

Q: Do you know from the start how a book will end?

A: No, but I do know that it is going to end, and that is a vitally important thing. I will have some ideas in my head right from the start. Then, when I'm five to ten thousand words into a book, I write the cover copy. It probably isn't the cover copy that the publisher is eventually going to require, but I write it anyway in order to tell myself what it is I think I'm thinking. If I can't summarize my story in 150 words, then what am I doing writing it?

Q: What do you tell young people who say they want to write?

A: Let grammar, punctuation, and spelling into your life! Even the most energetic and wonderful mess has to be turned into sentences. That is the hard job that, as a writer, you have to do yourself. You have to work at it. To be a writer, you also have to be a serious reader: to try to see how a book works, to always run ahead of the narrative to ask yourself, "Why is the author doing that?" You have to observe people on the street, to build up some idea of character. And you have to do it for yourself because you're going to be doing it in a different way from the last guy.

Q: What is the best part of being a writer?

A: Being my own boss—and having the sense of slight amazement that people are paying me a lot of money to do what I really, really want to do. I feel blessed—which is a very embarrassing position for an atheist to be in!

A TERRY PRATCHETT READER

The Bromeliad trilogy:
  Truckers (Doubleday, 1989)
  Diggers (Doubleday, 1990)
  Wings (Doubleday, 1990)

The Carpet People (Doubleday, 1992)

The Discworld series:
  The Amazing Maurice and His Educated Rodents
    (HarperCollins, 2001)
  The Wee Free Men (HarperCollins, 2003)
  A Hat Full of Sky (HarperCollins, 2004)
  Wintersmith (HarperCollins, 2006)

The Johnny Maxwell trilogy:
  Only You Can Save Mankind (HarperCollins, 2005)
  Johnny and the Dead (HarperCollins, 2006)

PHILIP PULLMAN

Born 1946, Norwich, England

ALTHOUGH BORN in England, Philip Pullman spent formative stretches of his childhood living far from home: first in Southern Rhodesia (now Zimbabwe), where his father, a Royal Air Force airman, was stationed and died in a crash; and later in Australia, his airman stepfather's posting. One result of these far-flung early travels may have been to make England itself seem as much an imaginary place as a real one to the daydreamy, thoughtful boy. A second result may have been to plant the seed for stories about journeys between worlds. In His Dark Materials, Pullman holds up to view the portion of England that he perhaps knows best—the historic university city of Oxford—through a beguiling double lens, depicting it both as an imposing, fortress-like center of learning and as a wraith-like gateway to mystery-laden, often treacherous other realms.

Pullman—or rather the part of himself he calls his "daylight mind"—enjoys reading about history, politics, social issues, and family relationships: all the things that people usually mean when they talk about "real life" and the opposite of "fantasy." As a writer, however, he feels most at home when telling stories involving an element of the "uncanny"—all the stuff left over after scientists have done their level best to explain everything. "The part [of my mind] that does the writing," Pullman says, "doesn't like the place cleaned up and freshly painted and brightly lit." *Real* real life is bound to be a bit messy.

Leonard S. Marcus: What kind of child were you?

Philip Pullman: An ingratiating little prig, I dare say! In my family, I was always considered the "dreamy, impractical one." It took me quite some time to realize that actually I'm not all that impractical—that, for example, I can make mechanical things work. Looking back, though, I suppose I was pretty well always more keen on reading a book than on doing anything else.

Q: What did you like to read?

A: Anything and everything, from ghost stories and Sherlock Holmes and modern detective stories, to fairy tales, to comic books.

In the 1950s it was very difficult to get hold of American comic books in Britain. "Horror comics," such as the series called *Tales from the Crypt,* were banned in Britain because some people thought them to be bad for children. The only kind we had were rather high-minded comics involving decent chaps being rather brave under difficult circumstances. But when I went to Australia at the age of eight or nine, suddenly American comic books—*Superman, Batman, Captain Marvel,* and others—were available to me, and I absolutely fell in love with them. I still love them.

Q: Was it the larger-than-life quality of Batman and Superman that appealed to you?

A: It was largely that to begin with. I also sensed that the comics were a new way of storytelling that didn't depend only on words, but also involved pictures that could move very quickly, snap at once from one scene to another with enormous economy and vividness. That was very exciting too. I was already keen on telling stories myself—retelling stories that I'd read in books to my friends and making them shiver!

Q: You were nine then?

A: About nine.

Q: When did you start writing stories?

A: I was already writing—creepy stories, ghost stories, and murder stories—mostly for my own benefit but also sometimes for school. Later on, in my teen years, I got rather more serious and started writing poetry. But the first impulse to write was a lurid, gaslit, story-telling impulse.

Q: Children who move frequently, as you did, often learn to size up other people rapidly. Was that true of you as a boy?

A: Yes. You make friends with people and then you have to leave and go somewhere else, and within the first morning in your new school, you come up against people who've known each other for years and years. You're the stranger, and you have to find a way of fitting in, which usually involves changing the way you speak, and your accent.

That is why Lyra's voice changes throughout the story. When, for instance, in *The Golden Compass* she goes to the Fens, among the Gyptian people, she finds herself almost unconsciously imitating the way they speak. You have to do that, and you have to work out quite quickly where the power lies in a new class of kids—because the power of course never lies with the teacher. It always lies with one or another of the other kids.

Q: Did you enjoy school?

A: Yes. I was quite quick at mathematics and English, and enjoyed getting praised for it. I liked the teachers, except for the ones who were brutal or impatient. I liked chasing girls, taking part in the school play, learning to smoke, just generally fooling about.

Q: Were there storytellers in your family?

A: My grandfather—my mother's father—was a priest in the Church of England, which is a very middle-of-the-road, nonzealous, neither-one-thing-nor-the-other church. He was a very middling member of that church—an ordinary priest. But to me then he was extraordinary because he was the only grandfather I had and he seemed to be the center of the family, the rock around which all the waters of accident and circumstance broke and retreated. And he was a storyteller.

I would go on walks with him as a little boy, and he would say, "Now we're going over this stream, boy, this little mill stream. This stream's called Laughing Water. I'll tell you why it's called Laughing Water. . . ." I didn't realize where he'd gotten the phrase "Laughing Water" until many years later, when I read Longfellow's poem *The Song of Hiawatha*. He just took the phrase and did something with it as a storyteller.

Philip Pullman,
age eleven

When he was a young man, he'd been to see Buffalo Bill's Wild West show when it was touring Britain, and it made a huge impression on him. He was a great one for the mythology of the old Wild West. He'd never been to America, but he seemed to know a lot about "cowboys and Indians."

Then there was a strange character called Gray Owl, who was a very big writer in the 1930s. Gray Owl purported to be a Native American, and he came to England and did lecture tours, and he told people about his "little brothers the beavers." He preached the wisdom of the "Red Man," as they used to say. He was a very impressive figure, this Gray Owl, with his noble profile and stories of living in the backwoods and paddling his canoe. A lot of the imagery in Grandfather's stories came from him, and it made a great impression on me and on all the other children my grandfather would speak to at the village school.

Q: Is there a little bit of Buffalo Bill, or Gray Owl, in your character Lee Scoresby?

A: Oh, I think so. I'm very fond of Lee. Gray Owl as it happens wasn't a Native American at all. He was an Englishman called Archie Belaney, and nobody knew this until he died.

Even so, Gray Owl wasn't a fraud—someone out to make money from people. He believed in what he was saying. He didn't believe he was telling the truth about himself, but he believed in the integrity of the message. So I think of him as really a good guy.

Q: Would you tell me about your teacher Enid Jones?

A: She was the English teacher in the school in Harlech, in North Wales, where I spent my teenage years. We moved there when I was eleven. It was a local school, nothing special about it except—this being Wales and not England—there was a commonly understood respect and value accorded to literature. The Welsh have the tradition of the Eisteddfod, which is a sort of cultural festival involving music and singing and the composition of poetry in Welsh. One of the teachers in my school won a prize for his Welsh poetry. Another was an amateur astronomer. Teachers were looked up to not only by the kids but also by their parents and everybody else around.

Something else that I've thought about lately is that my generation were taught by people who had served in the Second World War. Some of my teachers had served on the Arctic convoys, or been wounded while commanding tanks, or had flown solo missions ferrying planes across the Atlantic. These were men and women of some courage and moral stature. They had done something important in the world. They didn't make anything of this. Nobody said, "Let me tell you about my medals, boy." They themselves took it for granted, while we had the sense that they had been through something that made them bigger men than we would ever be. So, these were the teachers in the school.

Now Miss Jones was in her forties, a "spinster" as she would have been called then. She dedicated all her life to education. And she happened to teach my favorite subject, which was English. So naturally

I felt a kind of affinity with her. She was good enough to praise my stories when I had to write one for school. She would have me read them out to the class, which, I suppose, makes her my first publisher. Every year she would produce a play for the whole school that the parents would also attend. A big, big thing this was. I would always be first in the queue to audition. I remember all this with great affection. When I first published a book, I sent her a copy, and I have kept up this habit. We're still in touch. I like to feel that she's glad to see what I've done with the teaching she instilled in me.

Q: Did she read poetry aloud to the class?

A: That's right. One of the books we had to study was *Paradise Lost*. I found that many of the references made little or no sense to me. Nevertheless, the sound of Milton's poetry when heard read aloud, and then *tasted* afterwards in your own mouth, was enormously powerful. From that experience, I learned that things can affect us before we understand them, and at a deeper level than we can actually reach with our understanding. I also learned that you respond *physically* to poetry. Your hair stands on end. Your skin bristles. Your heart goes faster. Many years later, this was something I tried to teach the students I was involved in training to become teachers. The kids I was teaching were afraid of poetry. They thought that poetry was just a complicated way of saying something and that the children they were going to be teaching wouldn't like it because they would think it was complicated. So they thought the thing to do was to explain it, to "translate" it into simple language. I had to keep telling them, "When you do that, you take the poetry out of it. If you don't understand a poem, so what? Just listen to it. Just taste it.

Just say it. Just let it do its work without interfering with it. Sound first—then meaning."

Q: **You were a teenager, weren't you, when you turned away from religion. What led you to that decision?**

A: The reading I was doing. The American Beat poets: Allen Ginsberg, Lawrence Ferlinghetti, and Jack Kerouac. They were all rebelling, and I found that this was very attractive. I also read the philosopher Bertrand Russell and the playwright George Bernard Shaw, who both seemed to take it for granted that it was impossible to believe in an old-fashioned idea of God. I found I had to agree with them.

Q: **That must have been hard for you, especially given your admiration for your grandfather.**

A: It was difficult, but I didn't make a big thing of it and say, "Hey, I'm not going to church anymore. I'm going to rebel!" I knew that all that would be gained from that would be my grandfather's un-happiness, which I did not want to bring about. So I just carried on going to church, except I didn't believe it. I think there's too much attention paid to the urgency and importance of our own feelings and too little paid to the courtesy we owe to others.

Q: **Do you feel that that is when your childhood came to an end?**

A: That was part of it: growing away from the certainties of child-hood. And also doing the classic thing that everybody does as part of growing up, which is to discover what the differences are between themselves and the other members of the family. Our life begins at the moment we're born, but our life story begins at that moment when we discover we've been put in the wrong family by mistake!

Q: How did you choose the daemons for the characters of His Dark Materials?

A: Some I didn't have to choose. It was obvious what they should be. I knew that Mrs. Coulter's daemon was going to be a golden monkey. Monkeys for me have a kind of sinister quality to them. There's a wonderful ghost story by the Victorian writer Sheridan Le Fanu called "Green Tea." An apparition of an evil little monkey appears in that story, and it made a huge impression on me when I first read it as a child. Maybe the memory of that story was haunting me, and that's why it was so clear what Mrs. Coulter's daemon would be.

Q: Why does Lyra's daemon become a marten?

A: There is a painting by Leonardo da Vinci showing a young woman holding her pet, a ferret in its white winter coat—an ermine. I've always liked that picture. I make a habit of looking out for pictures of people, as it were, with their daemons. The da Vinci painting of the young woman seemed to me what Lyra would be like when she grew up. I called her daemon a pine marten because the words *weasel* and *stoat* and *ferret* don't sound very attractive. But they're all the same sort of creature.

Q: I was surprised you didn't choose a more heroic animal for your heroine.

A: Yes, but you see, a marten *is* Lyra-like. He can insinuate himself into all sorts of narrow spaces.

Q: You say Lyra does not have much of an imagination. That surprised me too.

A: I threw that in to make the reader think about the kind of stories Lyra tells. They are utterly conventional in every possible way. When she tells her fantasies—the first example of this comes in the "Suburbs of the Dead" chapter in *The Amber Spyglass*—when she tells the story to the family who are stuck in that ghastly shantytown, she entertains them, and she enjoys telling the story herself. But it is the most conventional fantasy story of adventure and excitement, without much input from her genuine heart or soul experience. A little later, of course, this becomes the crux when they're in the world of the dead and Lyra tries to tell that same story to the Harpies, who instantly recognize its falsity and fly at her with anger. It's only when she tells the truth—a real, truthful story—that she satisfies them. And that is what I meant to say: that imagination is not "making up strange things." Imagination is giving a true account of realistic things. I don't disparage the tales of Buffalo Bill and Superman and Batman, because they're very good practice for telling truthful stories.

Q: You must have thought about what your own daemon would be.

A: Not very much, actually. I suppose I think of her as a bird, probably one of those dull, drab-looking birds, like a jackdaw, which makes a habit of stealing bright things. She hangs around inconspicuously listening for little bright snippets of conversation or an anecdote and then picks them up when nobody's looking and brings them back to me, and we make a story out of them.

Q: When did you first read *The Lord of the Rings*?

A: When I was eighteen.

Q: J. R. R. Tolkien was still teaching at Oxford when you were a student there, wasn't he?

A: He was, indeed. I had dinner with him once.

Q: What was he like?

A: He was a genial old fellow in his seventies, world famous by then. The rector of our college—Exeter College, which had been Tolkien's

12 July 1998

Joan Slattery
Alfred A.Knopf
201 East 50th Street
New York, NY 10022
USA

Dear Joan,

Many thanks for the COUNT KARLSTEIN - how nice to see the
old boy so dressed up and still kicking! It looks very
handsome indeed, and the spot illustrations are a complete
delight.

And all is indeed well with the writing, writing, writing.
I do appreciate your forbearance - and David Fickling's too
- not many publishers would be so patient. I think I said
to you that the third book is going to be the longest, and
that's certainly being borne out by the way it's going. It
will be divided into three parts, like THE GOLDEN COMPASS,
of roughly 200, 250, and 150 pages each (those are my
written pages, which come down to a little less in print).
I knew from the beginning that my first task would be to
co-ordinate the various stories that are already going, and
deal with every strand separately, including the Dr Mary
Malone strand. In order to get that right I've had to have
the spotlight away from Lyra, who is in the power of Mrs
Coulter (unharmed - in fact in a drugged sleep) and show
how she is the focus of everyone else's activity. Will is
on his way to rescue her, of course; and it's on the way
there that he meets Iorek Byrnison. The main technical
thing was getting everything moving at roughly the same
speed and in the same direction, like a large team of
skittish horses all harnessed to a coach. But now they're
under my command, and each finger has a rein (if that's the
word) leading to a horse, and they're beginning to pick up
speed.

The story is going well, then. And what's more I've got the
underlying myth clear in my mind - I mean the animating
proposition, so to speak, about the world of the story. It
takes up a page or two. I might include that when I send
you the whole thing, to put in an appendix or something, as
you think fit.

Back to work!

All the best-

Yours
Philip

Letter from Philip Pullman to his American editor, Joan Slattery

college as well—invited me and a couple of my friends to dinner to meet the great man. I have to go back a bit and explain that it was Tolkien who fought the great battle to retain Anglo-Saxon as a subject of study at Oxford. Because he won that battle, every undergraduate had to read and study—and suffer—Anglo-Saxon.

And so we were all introduced and sat down to dinner. One of my friends was on one side of him; the other friend was on the other side. I was seated across the table. Professor Tolkien turned to the first fellow and said, "How are they pronouncing Anglo-Saxon these days?" That was one of the things the scholars argued over, you know: the different ways of pronouncing the wretched language! My friend had done as little work as I had, and had no idea. So he just sort of gaped and goggled and tried to make up an answer. Which displeased Tolkien, who turned to the other fellow and said, "Now then, young man, did you enjoy *The Lord of the Rings*?" My other friend had to say, "Well, I'm awfully sorry but I haven't read it." I could have answered *that* question, at least. But that was the end of Tolkien's conversation. He never got round to asking me anything.

The Lord of the Rings did make a big impression on me, as it did on everyone who read it in the 1960s. We all went about pretending to be Aragorn—and being hippies. I enjoyed the storytelling, the way the story moved so powerfully and grippingly onward. But I've only read it once. I tried to re-read it later but gave up because there's nothing that satisfies me in it now. It's the difference between Lyra's false story and her true story. There's nothing truthful in it about human nature, or society, or men and women. Nothing true in it at all. It's all superficial adventure.

Q: What writers have inspired you?

A: William Blake is a great inspiration, not least because of his cheerful indifference to the indifference of fortune. He would go on writing and engraving and living in poverty—as he did for all his seventy years—with utter cheerfulness. Not complaining. Not making a fuss. "Why aren't I famous? Wordsworth's famous. What's all the talk about this Shelley fellow? What about *me*?" He didn't do a bit of that, and I admire him for it!

Q: Was writing such a long work as His Dark Materials a lonely experience?

A: It was at the beginning, and during parts of the second book. But then it kind of caught on with the public and got more and more attention, and I became aware that I wasn't alone and that there were quite a number of people impatient and eager for me to finish. They used to write to me and tell me so with great frequency. It could have been distracting if I hadn't by this time become used to being ignored, and able to take no notice of what was going on outside, so that whether my work was greeted with total silence or with acclamation was all the same to me. It would have been much more difficult if I had been young, if this had been my first book.

Q: Did you have a plan for the three books from the start?

A: Not a plan. But I knew what the story was going to be and where it was going to go and when it was going to end, and roughly how long it was going to be. I didn't intend to write three books. I intended to write a long story. But it very quickly became evident that it would have to be published as three books because otherwise it would just sit on the shelves. It probably wouldn't have gotten published. Who would publish a thirteen-hundred-page-long book for children?

Q: Did you start writing at the beginning, with the scene set at Oxford, in which Lyra discovers the plot to poison Lord Asriel?

A: Yes, I started with the idea of the little girl going to the place where she shouldn't be. It's a dramatic situation. You're wondering if she's going to get caught. She overhears something that she shouldn't overhear and you wonder about the consequences of that. It was an opening that was hard to fail with.

Q: You taught twelve-year-olds for many years. Did you learn anything from that experience that has helped you as a writer?

A: I told my students lots of folktales, fairy tales, and mythological stories. I knew they probably wouldn't ever hear the story of the Trojan War, which is one of the great stories, unless I told it to them, so I told them the *Iliad* and the *Odyssey*. I did it for their benefit initially but soon realized that I was enjoying it a great deal as well. That was my apprenticeship as a storyteller.

Q: Do you have a daily work routine?

A: Not lately. I wish I did. The routine I hope to get back to is: Go into my study at about half past nine. Sit down at my table and write by hand for the whole of the morning, until about one o'clock, with a break for coffee and a break for getting out and stretching myself. Then return in the afternoon, the aim of the day being to complete about a thousand words, or three handwritten pages. Then I stop. That would be a day's work.

Q: In *The Golden Compass,* you say about Lyra, "Even a job like scrubbing a deck could be satisfying, if it was done in a seamanlike way. She was very taken with that notion." I have the feeling that you are too.

A: You can approach any task, even the dullest one, like washing dishes, and do it in a way that's better than other ways: simply and clearly and well. There's a satisfaction in doing something that way. And of course the same holds true for writing.

Q: What kinds of research do you do for your books?

A: I have an old friend, Michael Malleson, who is a blacksmith. When I was going to write about the Subtle Knife, I asked him to show me what is involved in the process of heating iron to the point that you can weld it with another piece of metal. He fired up the forge and heated the metal, and I got lots of little details about the glistening surface of the metal and the way the little sparks behave when they fly up. I couldn't have imagined such things accurately.

I'm passionately interested in all kinds of craftsmanship. I very much enjoy making things with my hands. As a matter of fact, I'm about to start making a rocking horse for my grandson. This is something in which I take a great deal of pleasure. And I think that if it's possible to do something well, then doing it well is a good thing.

Q: What do you do when you get stuck?

A: I sit and groan and scratch my head and tap my pencil on my chair. If you're determined to write three pages every day, you do. If you're stuck, you just write three bad pages. It doesn't matter. You got the work done. It's piled up. There are three pages there that weren't there yesterday.

Sometimes when there's a technical holdup in a story, I'll go and have a cup of coffee at the Oxford Museum of Modern Art café. I've got two things planned for my protagonist to do, but I can't decide which order they should come in. If I do them in *this* order, then *that* won't work, and if I do them in the other order, then something else won't work. That's the sort of problem I have when I go to the café and sit and think and write through the alternatives: the advantages of one and the disadvantages of the other. It very often does seem to work that I can find the best answer by being there. Curious!

Q: What is the best thing for you about being a writer?

A: There are many good things. Working when I want to. Not having to wear a tie. The freedom from having a boss.

A PHILIP PULLMAN READER

Clockwork, illustrated by Leonid Gore (Arthur A.
    Levine/Scholastic, 1998)

Count Karlstein, illustrated by Diana Bryan (Knopf, 1998)

His Dark Materials series:
    The Golden Compass (Knopf, 1996)
    The Subtle Knife (Knopf, 1997)
    The Amber Spyglass (Knopf, 2002)
    Lyra's Oxford, illustrated by John Lawrence (Knopf, 2003)

The Scarecrow and His Servant, illustrated by Peter Bailey
    (Knopf, 2005)

Spring-Heeled Jack: A Story of Bravery and Evil, illustrated by
    David Mostyn (Knopf, 1991)

JANE YOLEN

Born 1939, New York, New York

"AS A WRITER," Jane Yolen once said, "I am an empress of thieves, taking characters like gargoyles off Parisian churches, the *ki-lin* (or unicorn) from China, swords in stones from the Celts, landscapes from the Taino people. I have pulled threads from magic tapestries to weave up my own new cloth."

Just as varied as have been the sources of her writing are the forms her writing has taken over the years. In addition to fantasies, Yolen has written short stories, poems, essays, historical fiction, picture-book stories and retellings of folktales, and nonfiction ranging from a history of kite flying to a book about the Quaker religion. Her very first published book, *Pirates in Petticoats* (1963), was a collection of true stories about pirate woman adventurers. Her second book, published in the same year, was a picture book in rhyme called *See This Little Line?*

Yolen likes to perform her stories as well as to write them down in books because, as she once observed, "the eye and the ear are different listeners." She has edited poetry anthologies, co-authored novels with Bruce Coville and Robert J. Harris, and made a point throughout her career of helping younger writers get their start. Encouraging other writers is important to her in part because she believes that stories are like dreams or memories for everyone to contribute to and share. This being the case, a storyteller has two basic responsibilities: first, to "touch magic," and then to "pass it on."

Leonard S. Marcus: What kind of child were you?

Jane Yolen: I was a dreamy child. A reader. A little whiny. A performer. I was bossy to my brother. And I was very moral, which is probably why I love fantasy. In fantasy, you can talk about the great moral issues—honor, heroism, truth, trust, loyalty, and evil—things that become pretty clouded and gray in most modern "realistic" literature.

Q: Did you like to read as a child?

A: I learned to read at about the age of four. If a book was British and fantasy, I read it: T. H. White, E. Nesbit, *The Wind in the Willows*. I was really into Andrew Lang's "color" fairy-tale books. My parents had an encyclopedia with entries that were written in a story-like way. I started at the *A*'s and soon came to the entry for King Arthur. The King Arthur legend had *everything*: it was romantic; it was swashbuckling; it had honor, truth, love, and betrayal. I thought

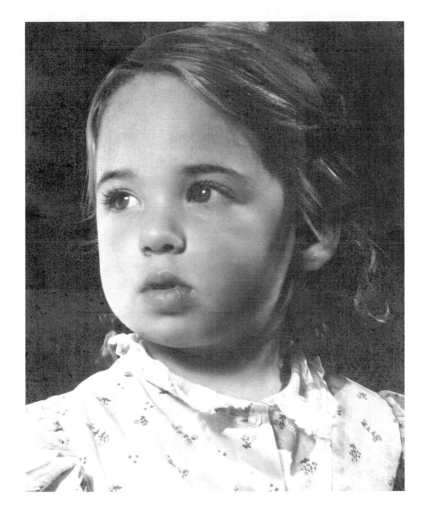

Jane Yolen,
about age two

it was the greatest story ever told. I was also a big Oz fan and read
every horse and dog book I could find.

Q: Were there storytellers in your family?

A: Everyone in my family was funny. And because both my parents
were writers, I thought that all grownups were writers. My mother
wrote short stories and created double acrostic puzzles. My father
was a newspaper man and then a public relations man as well as an
author. He did the publicity for Dubble Bubble bubblegum, Slinky,

and Silly Putty. Because of this, my brother and I were the first children on the block to have all of these great things—as much as we wanted. Every time our Slinky went down the stairs and became all tangled, we could have six more! We were photographed for bubblegum advertisements sitting on suitcases in Grand Central Terminal with big bubbles coming out of our mouths. This was well before "truth in advertising," and what we actually had in our mouths were big balloons. These photographs were published all across the country.

When my uncle Eddie, a physicist, introduced my father to Dr. Francis Rogallo, another physicist who wanted to go into business manufacturing kites for children's toys, Rog asked my father to do the publicity for him. That was how my father fell into kiting. Mind you, *I* never was able to get a kite up into the air. The family story was that after feeling embarrassed to be seen flying a kite without a child at his side, my father finally made a cardboard mockup of a child and propped it up on the lawn so that people driving by would say, "Oh, look at that good father. What an ugly child . . ."

Q: Is that a true story?

A: Like most Yolen family stories, I have no idea! But my father *did* become a world kite-flying champion. First, he became Western Hemisphere champion—simply by announcing that he was. Then one day he received a challenge from the maharajah of Burhanpur, in India, who claimed to be the Eastern Hemisphere champion. The maharajah sent my father two round-trip tickets to India and arranged to have a kite fight on the lawn of his hunting palace. My father was such a good publicity person that instead of bringing my mother along with him on this fabulous trip he took Red Smith, the great *New York Herald Tribune* sportswriter, so that Red could write about the kite fight. When it was all over, my father came home and declared himself the world champion. I'm sure that back in India the maharajah did the same.

Q: Do you remember World War II?

A: I knew about it, but I didn't know about it. I was about four or five when the war began. I was too young to make any connection between what was happening then and, for example, the battles fought by King Arthur. When my father, then a second lieutenant in the army, sailed off to England, we moved down from New York to

Virginia to stay with my mother's parents. So the war for me was the adventure of living with my cousins and watching the boats go off and not having my father around for two years.

Q: Did you like to write as a child?

A: I started writing in second grade. Even before then, I had written a couple of very bad little poems. But in second grade, I wrote our class musical. We were different kinds of vegetables, and we ended up in a salad together. I, being ever the overachiever, played the lead carrot! Our next project was to make a picture or a diorama of an imaginary place, and mine was called "Candy Cane Island." I even wrote music for a little song that went, "Where is the Candy Cane Island? / Where in the world can it be? / Right across dreamland, across the canal, / Just come and follow me." Pretty sophisticated for a second-grader.

Q: Did you already know you wanted to be a writer?

A: First I wanted to be a ballet dancer. Then I wanted to be a choreographer. For one summer I wanted to have a horse farm—until I spent two months cleaning horse stalls. That was the end of that. Then I thought about becoming a lawyer. For a while, I was going to be a folksinger or a Broadway musical star, but I just couldn't take the face-to-face rejections at auditions. If you are a writer and receive a rejection letter in the mail, at least you can kick the cat in private. Up through college, the two kinds of writing that I did were journalism and poetry. I assumed I was going to make my living as a journalist and my life as a poet. I became a performer after all, as I now enjoy doing storytelling performances and giving readings of my poetry and short fiction.

Q: Did you enjoy school?

A: I was always one of those gold-star kids who could do well even without studying. It was first at Hunter Junior High in New York City, and later at Smith College, that I discovered that there were certain subjects I wasn't the smartest in.

Q: Were there teachers, or other grownups besides your parents, from whom you learned a lot?

A: In high school there were three people. One was an older cousin, Honey Knopp, who was involved in the anti–Vietnam War movement and who liked to have folksingers over for "hootnannies" at her home. She helped to solidify my commitment to political activism, and she expanded my knowledge of folk culture. Then there was my English teacher, V. Louise Higgins, who was incredibly strong minded and made us read great literature—*War and Peace*, for instance. And my feeling for art as a part of everyday life was encouraged by my aunt Isabelle Yolen, who was an interior decorator.

Q: Why did you decide to write for children?

A: It really began as a happy accident. An editor who had heard about me from someone at Smith called one day and asked if I was working on a book. I told her that I was, just so that she would meet with me. In fact I wasn't working on anything at all. So then I had to come up with something in a hurry, and I had the idea that writing a children's book might be easy. I soon found out that that wasn't true.

Q: Why do you write about dragons?

A: I loved and rode horses as a child. I think of a dragon as a very large and amazing horse, or as a dinosaur brought into a different kind of focus. The mythic creature I probably identify most closely with, though, is the selkie. A selkie is two creatures in a single skin. If you put the skin on, you're a seal; if you take the skin off, you're a human. I think of writers and artists as being like that. One minute you are an ordinary person, and then you can put on the writer's skin and it allows you to go to magical places.

Q: Why is it that so many of your books are about a character remembering, or not remembering, something important?

A: One reason might be that because my life as a child was pretty easy, I have very little memory of my childhood. We know ourselves by the stories we tell about ourselves. If you can't remember the stories, then who are you? In *The Devil's Arithmetic,* Hannah *has* to become Chaya because she doesn't remember Hannah's story anymore. It's that "skin thing" again. She has to take on the other skin. And while she has that skin on, she has to dive into the waters and become a part of the story—and history—of her people.

Memory and story are related. When I write down something that happened to me, I am apt to change what happened to make a better story of it. Story revises memory to get at the truth. I've always loved the paradox that in storytelling you have to lie in order to tell the truth.

Q: Do you sometimes model characters on people you know?

A: Sure. Jakkin, from the Pit Dragon trilogy, for instance, is based on my son Adam, who has a blunt truthfulness about him and yet a naiveté that is very interesting. Like Jakkin, he has to discover things on his own. Adam is also Commander Toad. Akki, also from the Pit Dragon books, is feisty like my daughter, Heidi.

Q: What is it like to collaborate on a book with another writer?

A: It's different with each collaborator. I feel I always learn something

Jakkin caught up with the others at the bottom of the hill
where the jigsaw puzzle fields ~~half newly plowed and half~~
~~grown high with their crop of burnwort, came together.~~ Jakkin
assumed the lead, guiding them ~~as~~ along the hardpacked rows of wort
where ~~there~~ they would be less likely to leave footprints. He
was ~~careful~~ to skirt the smoking plants, warning Golden away
from the stalks that could burn at a touch. But even with the
warning, Golden's hands and his shirt bore the marks of ~~their~~ his

Akki ~~who had known previous lived a number of years on the~~
~~farm~~ managed better, ~~but even she~~ had one long burn along
her palm where she had held her hand up to shield her face.

~~Jakkin~~
~~the first~~
~~Once~~ past the fields, they had to wade ~~the best~~ across the
stone weir that channeled water from the Narakka River into
the Dragonry. The water was knee-high on Jakkin and Golden,
almost thigh high on Akki. But once they emerged from the ~~lake~~,
dike, the desert air dried their ~~shirtkkx~~ pants quickly. Another group
of fields, and another weir, and they were to the main road,
~~and still there was no sound of pursuit.~~
Jakkin
~~Golden~~ signalled a stop, and they squatted down in the dunes
near the road where they could see but not be seen, effectively
screened by the sand mound. Heat streamed off the road.
"I hear nothing," ~~Jakkin~~ said. "He must have put up
an incredible fight," he explained quickly.
Akki ~~shook her head~~ and held her left hand with her right.
The burn must have hurt, but she ~~said nothing~~ did not complain.

169.

from the people I write with. They move me in ways that I might be too timid to go on my own.

When Bruce Coville and I collaborated, we each created a different voice and character. But when I'm working with Bob Harris, he and I sit down and talk about our idea of the book, then he goes home and writes. He's much the better plotter than I am. I'm more into characters and scenes and landscape. He gets the characters wandering around—then I put their clothes on! So he sends me the first draft, chapter by chapter. As I receive each chapter, I shape it and add details and dialogue, often turning one chapter into two or three. Then he goes over it again, then I do.

Q: Why do you write about Scotland and live there part-time?

A: Several years ago, my husband, David, and I visited Scotland. When we got into the Highlands, we just looked at each other and said, "This is home!" Why I don't know. David has Scottish ancestry, but my ancestors were Jews from the Ukraine and Latvia. I love the sound of the Scottish language, the people, the fact that they take stones from old buildings and reuse them when they rebuild. I love the idea of reusing the past over and over. It's the opposite of America, where we throw away everything. We even throw away the past. I love the Scots' sense of having a living history.

Q: You write about that contrast in the Tartan Magic series.

A: In the second book, *The Pictish Child,* the girl saves her Scottish grandmother with the help of electricity. Afterward, the grandmother laughs and says, "You have electricity but we [the Scots] have power." The word *power* works two ways, of course, because that's what they call electricity.

Q: Do you have a daily work routine?

A: Yes. The magic word is BIC: butt in chair! I get up in the morning and I go to work. I stop to eat. That's what I do. This goes way back to my college days, when I was determined to do my own writing as well as my schoolwork. I had to be very disciplined, and ever since then I've been very good at finding little discrete packets of time all through the day and working intensely.

Q: Do you know from the start how a book is going to end?

A: No. I don't think I have ever written a novel that ended the way I thought it might end. Someone once called this way of writing "flying into the mist." I love that. As you're going along, it's wonderful to be surprised. That's as true for the writer as it is for the reader. I have many starts in my files for which I still haven't found the ending. I put them aside until something tells me it's time to take them out again.

Q: Do you revise your work much?

A: I love revision. Getting the first draft down is the hard part. When you are revising, you're going back, finding which parts really do work.

Q: Do you do research for your books?

A: Yes. Sometimes what I discover is fascinating. Other times, it becomes tiring and I just want to get on with the story. When that happens, I go back later and, in the case of the Scottish historical fantasy books for instance, find out what my characters should be wearing and eating.

Q: How do you know when a book is done?

A: I don't know. At some point you just have to say, "That's it!" It helps to know that I have an editor waiting to read what I've written.

Q: What do you tell children who want to write?

A: That first you have to be readers. Otherwise, you're just going to repeat all the stories that have already been written. From reading you can also learn how stories are put together and how characters grow and change. Then, once you are a reader, you have to write something every day. It's a muscle that has to be kept in working order. And finally, never let anyone tell you you're not any good. You're always going to get some rejections, so you have to have inside of you a sense that what you are doing is good and important.

Q: What is the best part of being a writer?

A: One best part is being able to work at my own pace and in my own time. A second is that because I write for children, I know that what I am doing is meaningful. I know I am changing lives in a good way, by getting children to read who didn't like to read before and by making people happy.

A JANE YOLEN READER

The Devil's Arithmetic (Viking, 1988)

The Here There Be books:

    Here There Be Dragons, illustrated by David Wilgus
        (Harcourt, 1993)

    Here There Be Unicorns, illustrated by David Wilgus
        (Harcourt, 1994)

    Here There Be Witches, illustrated by David Wilgus
        (Harcourt, 1995)

    Here There Be Angels, illustrated by David Wilgus
        (Harcourt, 1996)

    Here There Be Ghosts, illustrated by David Wilgus
        (Harcourt, 1998)

Pirates in Petticoats, illustrated by Leonard Vosburgh
    (David McKay, 1963)

The Pit Dragon trilogy:

    Dragon's Blood (Delacorte, 1982)

    Heart's Blood (Delacorte, 1984)

    A Sending of Dragons (Delacorte, 1987)

See This Little Line? (David McKay, 1963)

Sword of the Rightful King (Harcourt, 2003)

The Tartan Magic series:

    The Wizard's Map (Harcourt, 1999)

    The Pictish Child (Harcourt, 1999)

    The Bagpiper's Ghost (Harcourt, 2002)

Touch Magic: Fantasy, Faerie and Folklore in the Literature of
    Childhood (Philomel, 1981)

ACKNOWLEDGMENTS

My warm and hearty thanks to the thirteen writers who gave so generously of their time and attention, and to the following individuals and institutions for their help in assembling the many and varied elements that comprise this book: J. A. Burrow, Melanie Chang, Liz Crampton, Harold Farmer, Anne Hoppe, Elise Howard, Ruth Katcher, Phyllis Larkin, Alexander Limont, Tim Moses, Richard Pettengill, Joan Slattery, Sonya Sones, Dave Stemple, Heidi E. Y. Stemple, Jason Stemple, Charlotte Jones Voiklis, the staffs of the University of Minnesota, University of Oregon, and Wheaton College Libraries, and Paul Zakris. Special thanks go to my editors at Candlewick Press, Liz Bicknell and Deborah Wayshak, for their commitment to this project and for all their good work; to my agent, George M. Nicholson, for his friendship and guidance; and as always to my wife and our son.

PHOTOGRAPHY CREDITS

Pages 4 and 8: Alexander Limont, courtesy of Lloyd Alexander • Page 15: manuscript page from *The Iron Ring* copyright © by Lloyd Alexander, courtesy of Lloyd Alexander • Page 18: Richard Pettengill • Page 23: manuscript page from *The Folk Keeper* copyright © by Franny Billingsley, courtesy of Franny Billingsley • Page 24: courtesy of Franny Billingsley • Page 32: courtesy of Susan Cooper • Page 37: courtesy of Susan Cooper • Pages 40–41: notebook pages for *Greenwitch* copyright © by Susan Cooper, courtesy of Susan Cooper • Page 48: Sonya Sones • Page 53: courtesy of Nancy Farmer • Page 57: manuscript page from unpublished work copyright © by Nancy Farmer, courtesy of Nancy Farmer • Page 62: David Jacques, M.A. • Page 66: courtesy of Brian Jacques • Page 70: manuscript page from *Redwall* copyright © by Brian Jacques, courtesy of Brian Jacques • Page 76: courtesy of HarperCollins • Page 84: R. A. Jones • Page 90: Marian Wood Kolisch • Page 93: courtesy of Ursula K. Le Guin • Page 95: manuscript page from "The Days Before" copyright © by Ursula K. Le Guin, courtesy of Ursula K. Le Guin • Page 98: manuscript page from *A Wizard of Earthsea* copyright © by Ursula K. LeGuin, Ursula K. Le Guin Papers, Coll. 270, Special Collections and University Archives, University of Oregon, Eugene, Oregon • Page 102: Judith Petrovich • Page 108: courtesy the Madeleine L'Engle Papers, Wheaton College (IL) Special Collections • Page 116: Robert McFarlane • Pages 121 and 124: courtesy of Garth Nix • Pages 128–129: notebook pages for *Drowned Wednesday* copyright © by Garth Nix, courtesy of Garth Nix • Pages 134 and 138: courtesy of Tamora Pierce • Page 145: manuscript page from *Page* copyright © by Tamora Pierce, courtesy of Tamora Pierce • Pages 152 and 158: courtesy of Terry Pratchett • Page 166: Neville Elder • Page 171: courtesy of Random House • Page 177: letter from Philip Pullman to Joan Slattery, dated July 12, 1998, copyright © 1998 by Philip Pullman, courtesy of Random House • Page 178: courtesy of Random House • Page 184: Jason Stemple • Page 187: courtesy of Jane Yolen • Page 188: Heidi E. Y. Stemple • Page 193: manuscript page from *Heart's Blood* copyright © by Jane Yolen, reprinted courtesy of The Kerlan Collection, University of Minnesota

INDEX